WHOLE MEAL SALADS

100 Fresh, Delectable Recipes for Easy One-Course Entrees

NORMAN KOLPAS

CONTEMPORARY
BOOKS
CHICAGO

Library of Congress Cataloging-in-Publication Data

Kolpas, Norman.
  Whole-meal salads : 100 fresh, delectable recipes for easy
one-course entrees / Norman Kolpas.
    p. cm.
  Includes index.
  ISBN 0-8092-3995-7 (paper)
  1. Salads. I. Title.
TX740.K67 1992
641.8′3—dc20
                 91-46229
                 CIP

Published by Contemporary Books, Inc.
180 North Michigan Avenue, Chicago, Illinois 60601
Manufactured in the United States of America
International Standard Book Number: 0-8092-3995-7

CONTENTS

ACKNOWLEDGMENTS

In my years of writing and editing books about food, several colleagues have taught me a great deal about the world of salads. Foremost is Richard Olney, with whom I worked for five years on Time-Life's landmark series, "The Good Cook." His stylish, French-inspired approach to both composed and casually tossed salads showed me that there was a world far beyond the iceberg lettuce and hothouse tomatoes of my childhood.

I also owe thanks to my good friend John Sedlar, owner/chef of Bikini and Saint-Estèphe restaurants in, respectively, Santa Monica and Manhattan Beach, California; and to Michael McCarty, owner of Michael's in Santa Monica and New York City. Working with both of them on their cookbooks, I gained valuable insight into the many and varied ways in which contemporary chefs have elevated the salad to a main course of culinary distinction.

Thanks also are due to my valiant testers, who endured countless salad-based meals while I wrote this book: Hu Goldman; Caryn Landau; Evonne and Joseph Magee; Betsy, Matt, and Gannon Salinger; and Chuck Stewart and Mike Bartell. The most stalwart accomplices of all were my wife and son, Katie and Jacob, who sampled virtually every salad in this book and gave me moral support throughout the cooking and writing.

Los Angeles-based photographer Brian Leatart and foodstylist Norman Stewart collaborated on this book's stunning cover photograph. I've been privileged to work with both of them before, and I'm proud that they could contribute to this book.

Finally, heartfelt thanks are owed to the people at Contemporary Books. Nancy Crossman continues to earn my appreciation and respect for her wise and warm-hearted guidance. She suggested the idea for this book and saw it through its early stages. With the birth of Nancy's daughter, Katherine, Linda Gray stepped in to edit the book through to completion and proved always to be keen-minded, patient, understanding, and good-humored. Many of Linda's and Nancy's colleagues at Contemporary Books have also helped and encouraged me along the way on this and other books. My gratitude to all of you.

INTRODUCTION

As we move toward the twenty-first century, nothing less than a revolution is taking place in the way we prepare and eat salads. Until recently, salads for the most part had changed little from the role they had played in meals since Roman times, when *herba salata*—salted greens, sometimes also flavored with oil, vinegar, and herbs—first graced the formal table. Even when a salad moved from the sidelines to center stage, it seldom smacked of serious cuisine: usually it was chicken or tuna tossed with some chopped vegetables and mayonnaise to make a hasty lunch, and it was scooped into an avocado half if a touch of elegance was desired.

But today, the salad stands out as one of the most popular main-course menu choices—for a number of significant reasons. More than ever, people who love to cook and to dine out are aware of their health—reducing their intake of fat and calories while increasing the amount of fresh produce and fiber they eat. By all these criteria, main-course salads are outstanding menu choices.

Adding to the appeal of such salads is the ever-growing cornucopia of fresh, fabulous produce available in supermarkets, greengrocers, and farmers' markets. From salad leaves of incredibly varied hues, shapes, tastes, and textures to peak-of-perfection baby and fully grown vegetables, to tropical fruits of dazzling variety—new ingredient choices exist like never before to inspire salad artistry.

And the culinary world continues to become an ever-shrinking global village, in which everyone seems to be enjoying, discussing, and cooking Italian, French, Chinese, Japanese, Cajun, Thai, Moroccan, Indian, Caribbean, Indonesian, Scandinavian, Southwestern, Californian, and other distinctive cuisines—often intermingling the ingredients

1

and techniques of two or more disparate cultures to delightful effect. The salad bowl or plate, with its wide variety of ingredients, offers the ideal canvas for creating such multinational compositions. Many innovative chefs now gain acclaim for—of all things!—their salads.

Indeed, today's main-course salad couldn't seem further removed from that tuna-stuffed avocado. More likely than not, it begins with a bed of crisp young salad greens, arranged as beautifully as a bouquet. On top of that may go freshly cooked seafood, poultry, or meat, accompanied by complementary vegetables or fruits and a dressing as expertly tailored to the ingredients as any classic sauce of grand cuisine. It is, in effect, an entire, satisfying meal in a single dish—a logical selection for the busy, health-conscious, contemporary gourmet.

This book celebrates such whole-meal salads in all their delightful diversity. On the following pages you'll find information and guidelines for the fundamentals of whole-meal salad making: basic ingredients, including salad leaves, vinegars, oils, and frequently used embellishments, and instructions for arranging and serving your salads. This section is followed by seven chapters of whole-meal salad recipes. They are grouped by the main—you might say defining—ingredient of each salad: seafood, poultry, meat, cheese and egg, pasta and grain, vegetables, and fruits.

As you read through and cook from this book, you'll no doubt come up with your own ideas for new salad combinations. That, even more than offering you delicious, easy-to-follow recipes, is the real point of this book. Please use it as the starting point for your own happy explorations into the world of whole-meal salads.

A BRIEF GUIDE TO SALAD GREENS

Time was, salad meant iceberg lettuce—or, if you were really being gourmet about it, romaine. But times have changed. The wide variety of lettuces used in this book, and listed here, are available in most well-stocked supermarkets and greengrocers:

Arugula: see *Rocket.*

Belgian endive: These small, tightly packed heads of spear-shaped leaves have a refreshing, slightly bitter taste. For the finest flavor, choose specimens whose edges tend toward a yellowish- rather than a dark-green color.

Bok choy: Crisp and refreshing, this Asian cabbage-like vegetable—with elongated white ribs fringed in green—is increasingly available in U.S. markets.

Boston lettuce: see *Butter lettuce.*

Butter lettuce: Numerous varieties of this loose-leafed lettuce exist, including Boston, Bibb, and limestone. As the group name suggests, these tend to have a soft texture and mild, sweet flavor.

Cabbage: Pungently flavored and crisp of texture, cabbage adds variety and earthiness to salads. In addition to the familiar green, white, and red varieties, the elongated, frilly-leafed, pale-green-and-white napa cabbage is particularly appealing. Its sweet flavor and crisp texture go particularly well in Asian-inspired salads.

Chicory: see *Curly endive.*

Corn salad: see *Lamb's lettuce.*

Cos lettuce: see *Romaine lettuce.*

Curly endive: Also known as chicory and sometimes by its French name, *frisée,* this frilly leaf has a distinctively bitter flavor that offers nice contrast to rich salad ingredients. Select heads with a paler yellow-green rather than a darker green color; center leaves will have a milder flavor.

Frisée: see *Curly endive.*

Iceberg lettuce: For years iceberg reigned in salads, largely because it has few distinctive qualities to divide opinion. So mild as to be virtually flavorless, it nevertheless has a texture that, straight out of the refrigerator, is chillingly crisp. Don't dismiss it entirely; mixed with other greens, it can add another—if slight—dimension, particularly in chopped salads.

Lamb's lettuce: Also known by its French name, *mâche,* and as corn salad, these small, tender, sweet, velvety green leaves are said to resemble the shape of a lamb's tongue.

Limestone lettuce: see *Butter lettuce.*

Mâche: see *Lamb's lettuce.*

Oak leaf lettuce: These tender, mild, small to medium-sized leaves—either green or tinged with red—resemble the notched shape of an oak leaf. The term is also sometimes applied to red leaf lettuces.

Radicchio: Resembling miniature, elongated purple-red cabbages with white ribs, these leaves add bright color and a distinctively bitter flavor to salads.

Red chicory: see *Radicchio.*

Red leaf lettuce: An excellent all-purpose leaf with a crisp, cream-colored rib and soft, frilly, green edges trimmed in red, this lettuce combines a mild, sweet flavor with just a hint of bitterness.

Rocket: Often known by its Italian name, arugula, these small, lobed, dark-green leaves have a tart, peppery, slightly bitter flavor.

Romaine lettuce: Almost as crisp as an iceberg lettuce, this elongated leaf lettuce, also known as cos, has a more complex texture and assertive—though still relatively sweet—flavor.

Ruby lettuce: see *Red leaf lettuce.*

Spinach: With its strong, slightly astringent flavor and its tender—if somewhat coarse—texture, raw spinach has gained ever more popularity in the salad bowl. When using spinach, be sure to wash it thoroughly in several changes of water—lifting the leaves out of the water after each wash, before draining and rinsing the sink—to eliminate every last trace of sandy soil.

Watercress: Delightfully crisp and peppery, dark green watercress leaves are promoted with increasing frequency from the realm of garnishes to a starring position in salads.

MIXED BABY SALAD LEAVES

A number of the recipes in this book—particularly those of a more elegant or nouvelle-style slant—call for mixed baby salad leaves as their foundation.

Picked when only a few inches long, such leaves have a subtlety of flavor and tenderness of texture that can send a salad lover swooning. They're well worth seeking out—or growing yourself if you have a patch of ground and the time.

Many produce departments today carry mixed baby leaves, either loosely tossed together or prebagged and priced, which usually include such staples as butter lettuce, lamb's lettuce, rocket, curly endive, spinach, and red leaf lettuce—as well as any number of other additions.

In other cases, you'll have to select your own mixture of what's available. Just be sure to choose as widely varied an assortment as you can, selecting leaves that offer plentiful contrasts of color, shape, taste, and texture.

If baby greens are not available to you locally, choose instead the smallest regular specimens you can find, tearing them into large bite-sized pieces. If you care to splurge a little, use just the smaller inner leaves of the heads or bunches of greens you buy, reserving the outer leaves for another recipe.

STORING SALAD GREENS

Whatever salad greens you purchase, try to use them within two days of purchase to enjoy them at their peak of appearance, texture, and flavor. Before use, keep them in the vegetable crisper of your refrigerator, in perforated plastic bags or loosely wrapped in paper towels to allow air circulation.

SALAD ACCOMPANIMENTS

ROASTED PEPPERS

Oven roasting brings rich flavor and tender texture to peppers—qualities that make them a favorite ingredient of today's whole-meal salads.

To roast peppers, place on a baking sheet in a 500°F oven. Roast until skins are evenly blistered and browned, about 25 minutes, turning two to three times so they roast evenly. Remove from the oven and cover with a kitchen towel.

When peppers are cool enough to handle, pull out stems, peel away blackened skins, open peppers up, and remove seeds, using a teaspoon to pick up any strays.

A NOTE ON CHILI PEPPERS

Some of the recipes in this book call for fresh, canned, or roasted chili peppers. Take special care when handling them, as they contain oils that can cause a painful burning sensation upon contact with the eyes or the skin.

Use kitchen gloves, particularly if you have any cuts or abrasions or if your skin tends to be sensitive.

After handling chilies, wash your hands liberally with plenty of warm, soapy water.

Be very careful not to touch your eyes after handling chilies. If you do so accidentally, splash plenty of cool water in your eyes to rinse them.

CROUTONS

Crisp croutons add a crunchy contrast of texture—as well as the satisfaction of additional carbohydrates—to the salad bowl. While I've specified them in certain recipes in this book, you can feel free to add them to virtually any salad you like where they seem appropriate.

To make croutons, preheat the oven to 350°F. Brush ½- to ¾-inch-thick slices of slightly stale bread, with or without crusts, as you like, on both sides with enough olive oil, melted butter, or a mixture, to coat—using more or less according to your taste and diet. Cut slices into ¾-inch squares, spread in a single layer on a baking sheet, and bake, turning occasionally, until evenly crisp and golden brown, about 30 minutes.

For flavored croutons, add favorite seasonings to the oil or butter: a crushed garlic clove for garlic croutons, finely crumbled dried herbs (oregano, rosemary, thyme, savory, dill, and so on) for herb croutons, finely grated Parmesan for cheese croutons.

Store any extra croutons in an airtight container and use within a few days.

TOASTED NUTS

Just as croutons add their texture and flavor to salads, so do a wide variety of nuts make their own rich, crunchy contribution to the whole-meal salad bowl.

For salad-making purposes, it is best to start with plain shelled and blanched nuts that have not been roasted, salted, or otherwise cooked or seasoned in any way.

To toast nuts, preheat the oven to 325°F. Spread the nuts in a single layer on a baking sheet and bake just until light golden brown: 1 to 2 minutes for sesame seeds or shredded coconut, no more than 3 to 5 minutes or so for small nuts such as pine nuts or slivered almonds, and up to 10 minutes for larger, whole nuts. Be sure to check frequently to prevent the nuts from burning: they will continue to darken slightly after you remove them from the oven.

Once cooled, store toasted nuts in an airtight container to preserve their crispness.

CHOOSING OILS AND VINEGARS FOR SALADS

In most cases, oil-and-vinegar dressings are to the whole-meal salad what the sauce is to a traditional main course. The quality of the dressing ingredients you select will have a major impact on the final outcome of the salad.

OILS

Olive oil: Far and away the leading salad oil, olive oil carries with it the rich, sweet flavor of the fruit from which it is pressed. For salads, choose extra-virgin olive oil—extracted from olives on the first pressing without the use of heat or chemicals. Surveying the wide variety of such oils now available today, you'll notice a great range of colors. As a rule, darker, greener oils have more pronounced flavors. Start your own selection process by purchasing the smallest bottles possible, until you find an oil whose taste you prefer. Store airtight, away from light and heat.

Hazelnut and walnut oils: Some recipes in this book call for distinctively rich hazelnut and walnut oils to add an extra depth of flavor. Buy these oils in small quantities—they spoil rapidly—and store in airtight containers away from heat and light.

Sesame oil: Imported sesame oil, with its rich, dark, golden color, has a marvelously rich, nutlike flavor that adds an exotic touch to salads—particularly those with an Asian flair. Steer clear of pale yellow, refined domestic brands, which have little if any distinctive quality. Buy in small quantities, and store in an airtight container away from light and heat.

Peanut oil: Good-quality peanut oil has a hint of that nut's richness yet serves as a good all-purpose, nonassertive salad oil.

VINEGARS

Balsamic vinegar: Steeped with herbs and aged for years in wooden kegs, this red wine–based vinegar from Modena, Italy, has as much character as a fine old wine—a marvelous addition to certain elegant main-course salads.

Cider vinegar: Carrying a characteristic bite and sweetness of the apples from which it is made, cider vinegar adds a homey tang to dressings in which it is included.

Fruit vinegars: Some vinegars carry the distinctive character of a fruit wine—or the addition of fruit to a wine-vinegar base. Most notable among these—and most suitable, to my taste, for whole-meal salads—is good-quality raspberry vinegar.

Herb vinegars: Many supermarket gourmet sections now display a variety of vinegars flavored with bouquets of herbs, floating right in the bottle. To my taste, these flavors are usually too assertive; I prefer to add my herbs of choice to specific dressing mixtures. However, feel free to experiment with any flavored vinegars that might appeal to you.

Lemon juice: Though not a vinegar, lemon juice has just the right acidity to take vinegar's place—or enhance its impact—in many salad dressings. Perhaps it is needless to say in these sophisticated culinary times, but—you'll get the best flavor only if you use freshly squeezed lemon juice.

Rice vinegar: Imported from Asia, rice vinegar has a mild, sweet quality that makes it a natural for salads with a Chinese or Japanese accent.

Wine vinegars: Vinegars based on red or white wine are good all-purpose choices. But steer clear of inexpensive commercial wine vinegars, opting instead for higher quality products that actually began with good-quality wine whose character will shine through in the final product. Today, you'll even see vinegars that designate the wine varietal from which they are made—cabernet, chardonnay, and so forth. Have fun experimenting with them!

ARRANGING, DRESSING, AND SERVING THE WHOLE-MEAL SALAD

Dressing salads is very often a matter of individual taste: how much dressing you add, whether it is tossed before serving or by each guest, and so on. In the recipes in this book, I have tried wherever possible to offer options rather than straitjacketing you into one formula.

In most cases I have given dressing quantities that will yield a little more than you may actually need for any particular salad. That way, you have the option of adding more or less as your and your guests' tastes dictate. As a general guideline, though, count on 3 to 4 tablespoons of dressing for every 4 cups of salad greens.

As far as presentation goes, some of the salads are intended to be casually tossed before serving; others rely for their dramatic impact on a more precise arrangement of various ingredients—what is classically known as a composed salad. In such latter cases, however, I have tried not to make the instructions too precise: feel free to arrange the elements in a way that you find most pleasing. Where practical, I've also given you the option of serving salads from a platter or on individual plates.

A LOAF OF BREAD, A JUG OF WINE . . .

Good-quality bread is the only menu companion any of these salads really need to make a meal. Boutique-style bakeries are springing up all around the nation. Let me suggest that you seek out your best local ones and add even more variety to your table with fresh-baked loaves or rolls specifically chosen to complement your whole-meal salads.

And don't shy away from pouring a glass of wine with your salads. The old dictum that you can't serve a wine with salad hearkens back to the era of vinegary bowls of greens served between courses. The salads in this book have a depth and subtlety to them that calls out for a glass of wine that complements the featured ingredients—a cool white wine to go with the seafood, poultry, vegetable, or fruit salads, for example, or a hearty red with meat salads. Alternatively, you might want to pour a glass of beer to accompany a robust, informal salad. Let your tastebuds, and your imbibing habits, be your guide!

A NOTE ON SERVING QUANTITIES

As you'll see while flipping through the recipes, I've designated them as yielding "4 generous servings" each. Remember: This is a book on main-course salads. Each recipe is meant to be a filling, satisfying meal in itself. If you have a lighter appetite or plan on using these recipes as part of a more elaborate menu, adjust the quantities or yields accordingly.

1

SEAFOOD SALADS

Classic Salade Niçoise with Grainy Dijon Mustard Vinaigrette

Seared Ahi Tuna Niçoise with Miniature Vegetables
and Creamy Dijon Mustard Vinaigrette

Italian Tuna, Sweet Onion, and White Bean Salad on a Bed of Bitter Greens

Tuna Mexicana with Jicama, Avocado, Chilies, Corn Chips,
and Cool and Spicy Rancho Dressing

Grilled Salmon Teriyaki Salad with Lamb's Lettuce
and Lemon-Sesame-Ginger Dressing

Miso-Grilled Salmon with Cucumber Sunomono Salad

Shrimp Cobb with a Light Lemon Herb Vinaigrette

Grilled Shrimp with Lemon Dill Caesar Salad

Caribbean Grilled Shrimp and Pepper Salad with Mango Pineapple Vinaigrette
on a Bed of Baby Greens

Thai-Style Grilled Shrimp with Tart and Tangy Salad

Griddled Crab Cakes with Chive Crème Fraîche and Salmon Caviar
on Watercress and Mixed Baby Salad Leaves with Ginger Lime Vinaigrette

Crab Salad with Apple and Pear, Plumped Raisins, Celery, Pecans,
and Curried Herb Mayonnaise

Seafood Louis

Sautéed Bay Scallop Salad with
Roasted Peppers and Pine Nuts on Baby Spinach

Chilled Poached Lobster Salad
with Salmon Caviar and Lemon Dill Cream Dressing

California-Style Grilled Lobster Salad with Golden Tomatoes, Roasted Peppers,
Avocado, and Sun-Dried Tomato Pesto Vinaigrette

Southwestern Seviche on a Bed of Baby Greens

Classic Salade Niçoise
with Grainy Dijon Mustard Vinaigrette

One of France's greatest contributions to the world of salads is here faithfully rendered in all its glory. Look for the olive oil–packed variety of tuna, usually imported from Italy and available in Italian delis and well-stocked supermarkets; it has a wonderful flavor. But if you're watching your calories, it's OK to substitute a good water-packed tuna.

GRAINY DIJON MUSTARD VINAIGRETTE

2 tablespoons red-wine vinegar
2 tablespoons lemon juice
2 tablespoons coarse-grained Dijon-style mustard
½ teaspoon salt
½ teaspoon white pepper
½ teaspoon sugar
¾ cup olive oil

SALAD

4 cups coarsely torn romaine lettuce leaves
4 cups coarsely torn oak leaf lettuce leaves
4 cups coarsely torn Bibb lettuce leaves
3 (6-ounce) cans Italian-style tuna packed in olive oil, drained
¾ pound green beans, topped, tailed, boiled until tender-crisp, and cooled
12 anchovy fillets, drained
8 or 12 (depending on size) small new potatoes, boiled until tender, cooled, and cut into quarters

4 hard-boiled eggs, quartered lengthwise
4 firm ripe Roma tomatoes, cored and quartered
1 large red bell pepper, halved, stemmed, seeded, and cut crosswise into thin strips
2 medium-sized beets, boiled until tender-crisp, cooled, peeled, and cut into ¼-inch-thick slices
¾ cup marinated black Niçoise-style olives
2 tablespoons finely chopped fresh chives
2 tablespoons finely chopped fresh Italian parsley

12

1. *Make vinaigrette:* In a mixing bowl, stir together vinegar, lemon juice, mustard, salt, pepper, and sugar. Whisking continuously, very slowly pour in oil until blended. Set aside.

2. *Arrange salad:* On a platter, individual plates, or shallow salad bowls, arrange lettuces in a bed. Break tuna into large chunks and scatter in center of lettuces. Around tuna, decoratively arrange green beans, anchovies, potatoes, eggs, tomatoes, pepper, beets, and olives. Garnish with chives and parsley. Pass dressing on the side.

MAKES 4 GENEROUS SERVINGS

Seared Ahi Tuna Niçoise with Miniature Vegetables and Creamy Dijon Mustard Vinaigrette

Everything about this haute version of a Niçoise salad has been elevated at least a notch, from the delicate baby greens to the miniature vegetables to the tuna fillet—grilled fashionably medium-rare—that they surround.

CREAMY DIJON MUSTARD
VINAIGRETTE
2 tablespoons balsamic vinegar
2 tablespoons lemon juice
2 tablespoons creamy Dijon-style mustard
½ teaspoon salt
½ teaspoon white pepper
½ teaspoon sugar
¾ cup olive oil

SEARED AHI TUNA
3 tablespoons lemon juice
3 tablespoons olive oil
2 tablespoons dried oregano
4 fillets fresh ahi tuna, 6 ounces each
Salt
White pepper

SALAD
12 cups mixed baby salad leaves (see Index)
¾ pound thin baby haricots verts (French green beans), boiled until tender-crisp and cooled
16 baby golden or red beets, 1 inch of tops left on, boiled until tender, cooled, and cut lengthwise into halves
16 baby golden or red plum tomatoes
12 anchovy fillets, drained
8 or 12 (depending on size) small yellow Finnish potatoes, boiled until tender, cooled, and cut into quarters
12 hard-boiled quail eggs, left whole, *or* 4 hard-boiled hen eggs, quartered lengthwise
1 large red bell pepper, roasted, stemmed, peeled, seeded (see Index), and torn into thin strips
1 large yellow bell pepper, roasted, stemmed, peeled, seeded (see Index), and torn into thin strips
¾ cup marinated black Niçoise-style olives
2 tablespoons finely chopped fresh chives
2 tablespoons finely chopped fresh chervil

1. *Make vinaigrette:* In a mixing bowl, stir together vinegar, lemon juice, mustard, salt, pepper, and sugar. Whisking continuously, very slowly pour in oil until blended. Set aside.

2. *Marinate tuna:* In a shallow dish, stir together lemon juice, oil, and oregano, and turn tuna fillets in mixture to coat. Marinate at room temperature for 15 to 30 minutes.

3. *Grill tuna:* Heat grill or broiler until very hot. Season tuna with salt and white pepper and grill until nicely seared and medium-rare to medium, 3 to 4 minutes per side.

4. *Arrange salad:* While tuna is grilling, arrange leaves in attractive patterns on individual plates. Place whole grilled tuna fillet at the center of each plate. Around and overlapping it, decoratively arrange haricots, beets, tomatoes, anchovies, potatoes, eggs, pepper strips, and olives. Garnish with chives and chervil. Pass dressing on the side.

MAKES 4 GENEROUS SERVINGS

Italian Tuna, Sweet Onion, and White Bean Salad on a Bed of Bitter Greens

One of my favorite Italian appetizers—tuna with white beans and sweet onion—inspired this simple, lively salad. You can find olive oil–packed tuna—usually imported from Italy—in Italian delis or well-stocked supermarkets.

LIGHT LEMON HERB VINAIGRETTE

¼ cup lemon juice
1 tablespoon finely chopped fresh dill
1 tablespoon finely chopped fresh Italian parsley
1 teaspoon creamy Dijon-style mustard
½ teaspoon salt
½ teaspoon white pepper
½ teaspoon sugar
½ cup plus 2 tablespoons olive oil

SALAD

1 large sweet Maui, Vidalia, or Walla Walla onion, or red onion, sliced thin
4 cups coarsely torn radicchio leaves
4 cups Belgian endive leaves cut crosswise into ¼-inch-wide pieces
4 cups whole small rocket leaves
3 cups canned Italian white beans, rinsed and drained
3 (6-ounce) cans Italian-style tuna packed in olive oil, drained
Cracked black pepper
2 ounces block Parmesan cheese, cut into thin shavings with a vegetable peeler or a small, sharp knife
2 tablespoons finely chopped fresh chives
2 tablespoons finely shredded fresh basil

1. *Make dressing and marinate onion:* In a mixing bowl, stir together lemon juice, herbs, mustard, salt, pepper, and sugar. Whisking continuously, slowly pour in oil until blended. Toss sliced onion in dressing and set aside to marinate 1 to 2 hours. Lift out onion and reserve along with dressing.

2. *Arrange salad:* In a mixing bowl, toss salad leaves with just enough dressing to coat; arrange in a bed on a platter or individual serving plates. Toss beans with remaining dressing and spread in center of leaves. Break tuna into coarse chunks on top of beans and strew with marinated onions. Season to taste with cracked pepper. Scatter on Parmesan shavings and garnish with chives and basil.

MAKES 4 GENEROUS SERVINGS

Tuna Mexicana with Jicama, Avocado, Chilies, Corn Chips, and Cool and Spicy Rancho Dressing

This casual, quickly prepared salad is a great alternative to the traditional deli-style tuna salad on a bed of lettuce. The dressing is a spicy variation on the familiar buttermilk-based ranch concoction.

COOL AND SPICY RANCHO DRESSING

¾ cup plus 2 tablespoons buttermilk
2½ tablespoons lime juice
1 tablespoon finely chopped cilantro
1 tablespoon finely chopped fresh chives
1 jalapeño chili, roasted, stemmed, peeled, seeded (see Index), and chopped fine
1 teaspoon coarse-grained Dijon-style mustard
½ teaspoon salt
½ teaspoon white pepper
½ teaspoon sugar

SALAD

3 (6-ounce) cans chunk albacore tuna, drained and flaked coarse
6 cups coarsely torn romaine lettuce leaves
6 cups coarsely torn iceberg lettuce leaves
1 cup coarsely shredded jicama
1 cup small-sized corn chips
6 tablespoons canned chopped mild green chilies
1 large firm ripe Haas avocado
2 ounces sharp cheddar cheese, shredded
2 ounces Monterey Jack cheese, shredded
Cilantro sprigs

1. *Make dressing:* Put all dressing ingredients in a container with a tight-fitting lid. Shake well.

2. *Toss salad:* Put all ingredients except avocado, cheese, and cilantro in a large mixing bowl. Halve, pit, peel, and coarsely chop avocado and add to bowl. Toss ingredients lightly but thoroughly with enough dressing to coat. Mound on serving plates, scatter shredded cheese on top, and garnish with cilantro.

MAKES 4 GENEROUS SERVINGS

Grilled Salmon Teriyaki Salad with Lamb's Lettuce and Lemon-Sesame-Ginger Dressing

Delicate leaves of lamb's lettuce, mixed with unusual contrasting garnishes and tossed in a light yet exotically flavored dressing, provide a lovely background for fillets of teriyaki-glazed salmon.

LEMON-SESAME-GINGER DRESSING

¼ cup soy sauce
2 tablespoons lemon juice
2 tablespoons rice vinegar
1½ tablespoons finely grated fresh gingerroot
1 tablespoon sesame seeds, toasted (see Index)
2 teaspoons sugar
½ teaspoon dry mustard
½ cup peanut oil
¼ cup sesame oil

GRILLED SALMON TERIYAKI

4 salmon fillets, 6 ounces each
¾ cup good-quality bottled teriyaki sauce

SALAD

Peanut oil for deep frying
4 packaged square Chinese wonton skins, cut into ¼-inch-wide strips
10 cups lamb's lettuce leaves
12 large dried shiitake mushrooms, soaked in warm water for 15 minutes, stems removed, caps cut into ¼-inch-wide slices
16 ears canned or bottled baby corn
2 tablespoons black sesame seeds
¼ cup pickled Japanese ginger, cut into thin slivers
½ cup mustard cress or alfalfa sprouts
1 lemon, cut into 4 wedges

1. *Make dressing:* In a container with a tight-fitting lid, stir together soy sauce, lemon juice, vinegar, ginger, sesame seeds, sugar, and mustard until well combined. Add peanut and sesame oils; cover and shake well. Set aside.

2. *Marinate salmon:* In a shallow dish, coat salmon fillets with teriyaki sauce and marinate at room temperature for 15 to 30 minutes.

3. *Fry wonton strips:* In a heavy skillet or wok, heat 1 to 2 inches of oil until very hot. Add wonton strips—in 2 or 3 batches if necessary, to prevent overcrowding—and fry until crisp and golden, 2 to 3 minutes. Remove with slotted spoon or wire skimmer and drain on paper towels.

4. *Cook salmon:* Heat grill or broiler until very hot. Lift salmon from sauce and grill until nicely browned, 4 to 5 minutes per side.

5. *Arrange salad:* Just before salmon is done, in a large mixing bowl, toss together lamb's lettuce, wonton strips, shiitake mushrooms, and baby corn with enough dressing to coat. Arrange in a bed on individual serving plates. Place a salmon fillet at the center of each plate and sprinkle with black sesame seeds, then pickled ginger slivers. Scatter mustard cress or sprouts around each fillet. Place a lemon wedge beside each fillet, for guests to squeeze over salmon.

MAKES 4 GENEROUS SERVINGS

Miso-Grilled Salmon
with Cucumber Sunomono Salad

This Japanese-inspired combination offers vivid flavors in a strikingly minimalist setting. Grilled salmon fillets are glazed with a rich miso (soybean paste) and served atop a traditional *sunomono* salad—a cool bed of thinly sliced cucumbers marinated in rice vinegar.

SUNOMONO SALAD
¼ cup Japanese rice vinegar
1 teaspoon sugar
1 teaspoon salt
2 medium-sized Japanese
  cucumbers, sliced paper-thin

MISO-GRILLED SALMON
6 tablespoons Japanese yellow
  miso (soybean paste)
2 tablespoons soy sauce
1 tablespoon finely grated fresh
  gingerroot
4 salmon fillets, 6 ounces each

SALAD
24 baby Bibb lettuce leaves
2 tablespoons black or white
  sesame seeds
¾ cup enoki mushrooms or
  thinly sliced small field
  mushrooms
6 tablespoons daikon (Japanese
  radish) sprouts

1. *Marinate cucumbers:* In a large glass or ceramic bowl, stir together rice vinegar, sugar, and salt. Add sliced cucumbers, mix well, cover, and refrigerate 3 to 4 hours.

2. *Marinate salmon:* In a shallow dish, stir together miso, soy sauce, and ginger, and turn salmon fillets in mixture to coat. Marinate at room temperature for 15 to 30 minutes.

3. *Cook salmon:* Heat grill or broiler until very hot. Lift salmon from sauce and grill until nicely browned, 4 to 5 minutes per side.

4. *Arrange salad:* While salmon is cooking, arrange Bibb lettuce leaves in neat beds on individual serving plates. Arrange cucumber slices neatly in center of each plate and sprinkle with sesame seeds. Place salmon fillets on top and scatter mushrooms around each fillet. Garnish fillets with daikon sprouts.

MAKES 4 GENEROUS SERVINGS

Shrimp Cobb with a Light Lemon Herb Vinaigrette

More and more, this seafood version of the favorite salad has been finding its way onto menus. In this version, individual servings are presented with the ingredients neatly arranged, on top of the greens, ready for each diner to dress and mix to taste.

LIGHT LEMON HERB
VINAIGRETTE
See Index

SALAD

12 cups coarsely chopped romaine
  lettuce leaves
1½ pounds cooked and shelled bay
  shrimp
8 slices streaky smoked bacon, fried crisp
  and crumbled coarse
6 firm ripe Roma tomatoes, stemmed,
  seeded, and chopped coarse

4 hard-boiled eggs, halved, yolks and
  whites separated, and chopped fine
6 ounces blue cheese, crumbled
4 medium-sized firm ripe Haas
  avocados
2 tablespoons finely chopped fresh dill

1. *Make dressing:* See Index for Light Lemon Herb Vinaigrette.

2. *Arrange and serve salad:* In large individual salad bowls, arrange beds of romaine. In neat rows on top of lettuce, arrange shrimp, bacon, tomatoes, eggs, and blue cheese, leaving room for avocado. Just before serving, halve, pit, and peel avocados and cut into ½-inch chunks; arrange on top of salads. Garnish with dill. Pass dressing on the side.

MAKES 4 GENEROUS SERVINGS

Grilled Shrimp with Lemon Dill Caesar Salad

Here is a light seafood version of the salad classic.

LEMON DILL CAESAR DRESSING
4 anchovy fillets
2 medium-sized garlic cloves, crushed
3 tablespoons lemon juice
1½ tablespoons finely chopped fresh dill
1 tablespoon white-wine Worcestershire
   sauce
1 large egg
½ cup olive oil

GRILLED SHRIMP
2 pounds raw medium-sized shrimp,
   shelled and deveined, tails left on
2 tablespoons lemon juice
2 tablespoons olive oil
Salt
White pepper

SALAD
14 cups coarsely torn romaine lettuce
   leaves, chilled in the refrigerator
2 cups garlic croutons (see Index)
6 tablespoons freshly grated Parmesan
   cheese
2 tablespoons finely chopped fresh
   chives

1. *Make dressing:* Bring a small saucepan of water to a boil. Meanwhile, in a shallow mixing bowl, mash together anchovies and garlic with a fork or the back of a spoon until smooth. Stir in lemon juice, dill, and Worcestershire. Drop egg into boiling water; boil 50 seconds, rinse under cold running water, and break into mixing bowl. Whisking constantly, slowly pour in oil until blended. Set aside.

2. *Marinate and grill shrimp:* In a bowl, toss shrimp with lemon juice and oil and marinate about 15 minutes. Meanwhile, heat grill or broiler until very hot. Sprinkle shrimp with salt and pepper and grill until done, 1 to 1½ minutes per side.

3. *Arrange salad:* Toss romaine, croutons, and Parmesan with enough dressing to coat well. Arrange in beds on individual plates. Place shrimp on top. Garnish with chives.

MAKES 4 GENEROUS SERVINGS

Caribbean Grilled Shrimp and Pepper Salad with Mango Pineapple Vinaigrette on a Bed of Baby Greens

The presence in this salad of two popular tropical fruits—marinated briefly as part of the dressing—gives it a delightfully exotic flavor.

MANGO PINEAPPLE VINAIGRETTE
¾ cup olive oil
½ cup finely chopped fresh mango
½ cup finely chopped fresh pineapple
¼ cup lime juice
½ teaspoon salt
½ teaspoon white pepper

CARIBBEAN GRILLED SHRIMP
AND PEPPERS
2 pounds raw medium-sized shrimp, shelled and deveined, tails left on
2 tablespoons lime juice
2 tablespoons olive oil
Salt
White pepper
1 red bell pepper, halved, stemmed, and seeded, each half cut into 4 wedges
1 yellow bell pepper, halved, stemmed, and seeded, each half cut into 4 wedges

SALAD
12 cups mixed baby salad leaves (see Index)
2 tablespoons finely chopped cilantro

1. *Make dressing:* In a mixing bowl, stir all ingredients together until well combined. Cover and refrigerate.

2. *Marinate shrimp:* In a mixing bowl, toss shrimp with lime juice and olive oil; marinate at room temperature for 15 minutes.

3. *Grill shrimp and peppers:* Preheat grill or broiler until very hot. Sprinkle shrimp with salt and pepper and grill with peppers until shrimp are done and peppers are slightly charred, 1 to 1½ minutes per side.

4. *Toss and arrange salad:* While shrimp are grilling, strain pineapple and mango from dressing, reserving both liquid and solids. Toss fruit with baby greens and just enough of dressing to coat. Arrange in beds on individual serving plates. Arrange shrimp and peppers on top and garnish with cilantro.

MAKES 4 GENEROUS SERVINGS

Thai-Style Grilled Shrimp with Tart and Tangy Salad

Though some of the ingredients sound exotic, all are available at well-stocked Asian markets.

TART AND TANGY DRESSING
½ cup peanut oil
¼ cup lime juice
2 tablespoons nam pla (Thai fish sauce)
1½ tablespoons sugar
½ teaspoon black pepper

GRILLED SHRIMP
1 large stalk lemon grass, shredded fine
1 garlic clove, crushed
2 tablespoons peanut oil
2 tablespoons lime juice
2 tablespoons finely chopped cilantro
1 tablespoon grated fresh gingerroot
2 pounds raw medium-sized shrimp,
    shelled and deveined, tails left on

SALAD
3 cups coarsely torn iceberg lettuce
    leaves
3 cups coarsely torn romaine lettuce
    leaves
3 cups thoroughly washed, stemmed,
    and coarsely torn spinach leaves
4 baby bok choy, chopped coarse
2 medium-sized carrots, shredded coarse
1 small red onion, halved lengthwise
    and sliced thin
½ Japanese cucumber, sliced thin, *or* 2
    large pickling cucumbers, sliced thin
½ cup coarsely chopped cilantro

1. *Make dressing:* Put all dressing ingredients in a container with a tight-fitting lid. Shake well. Set aside.

2. *Marinate shrimp:* In a mixing bowl, stir together lemon grass, garlic, peanut oil, lime juice, cilantro, and ginger. Toss shrimp with the mixture and marinate at room temperature for 30 minutes.

3. *Grill shrimp:* Preheat grill or broiler until very hot. Grill shrimp until done, 1 to 1½ minutes per side.

4. *Dress and arrange salad:* In a large mixing bowl, toss lettuces, spinach, bok choy, carrots, onion, and cucumber with enough dressing to coat. Arrange on a platter or individual serving plates and place shrimp on top. Garnish with cilantro.

MAKES 4 GENEROUS SERVINGS

Griddled Crab Cakes with Chive Crème Fraîche and Salmon Caviar on Watercress and Mixed Baby Salad Leaves with Ginger Lime Vinaigrette

Though the combination sounds involved, every step is very simple—and the results are elegant and rewarding.

GINGER LIME VINAIGRETTE
¼ cup lime juice
2 tablespoons finely grated fresh gingerroot
½ teaspoon salt
½ teaspoon white pepper
½ teaspoon sugar
¾ cup olive oil

GRIDDLED CRAB CAKES
1½ pounds cooked crabmeat, flaked and picked clean of shell and cartilage
1 egg, well beaten
½ cup mayonnaise
½ cup fine fresh bread crumbs
¼ cup heavy cream, chilled
¼ cup finely chopped fresh parsley
1 tablespoon fresh lemon juice
½ teaspoon salt
½ teaspoon black pepper
½ teaspoon paprika
½ cup olive oil
¼ cup all-purpose flour

SALAD
6 cups mixed baby salad leaves (see Index)
6 cups watercress sprigs
1 red bell pepper, roasted, stemmed, seeded (see Index), and torn into long, thin strips
1 yellow bell pepper, roasted, stemmed, seeded (see Index), and torn into long, thin strips
¼ cup crème fraîche
2 tablespoons finely chopped fresh chives
¼ cup salmon roe or golden caviar

1. *Make dressing:* In a bowl, stir together lime juice, ginger, salt, pepper, and sugar. Whisking continuously, slowly stir in olive oil until blended. Set aside.

2. *Mix and chill crab cakes:* In a mixing bowl, stir together crabmeat, egg, mayonnaise, bread crumbs, cream, parsley, lemon juice, salt, pepper, and paprika. Shape mixture into 12 round cakes about ¾ inch thick and place on a baking sheet lined with waxed paper. Cover and refrigerate 1 to 2 hours.

3. *Cook crab cakes:* In 2 large skillets, heat oil over moderate heat. Lightly dust crab cakes with flour on both sides and fry until golden, 3 to 5 minutes per side. Drain on paper towels.

4. *Toss and arrange salad:* In a mixing bowl, toss baby greens with just enough dressing to coat. Arrange greens in attractive patterns on individual serving plates. In bowl, toss watercress with more dressing to coat. Arrange in flattened mounds in the center of each plate. Place 3 crab cakes on top of watercress on each plate, strewing pepper strips around them. Stir together crème fraîche and chives and spoon a dollop on each crab cake; top with a small dollop of salmon roe or caviar.

MAKES 4 GENEROUS SERVINGS

Crab Salad with Apple and Pear, Plumped Raisins, Celery, Pecans, and Curried Herb Mayonnaise

This is a lively, flavored version of a classic creamed crabmeat salad.

CURRIED HERB MAYONNAISE
1 cup mayonnaise
2 tablespoons finely chopped fresh
  chives
2 tablespoons finely chopped cilantro
1 tablespoon medium-dry sherry
1 teaspoon curry powder

SALAD
¼ cup medium-dry sherry
¼ cup seedless golden or brown raisins
1½ pounds cooked crabmeat, flaked and
  picked clean of shell and cartilage
2 large celery stalks, cut crosswise into
  ¼-inch slices
2 small tart green eating apples, cored, 1
  chopped into ½-inch pieces, 1 cut into
  thin vertical slices and tossed with 2
  tablespoons lemon juice
1 small firm pear, cored and chopped
  into ½-inch pieces
½ cup coarsely chopped pecans, toasted
  (see Index)
24 small whole Bibb lettuce leaves
12 pecan halves, toasted (see Index)
Cilantro sprigs

1. *Make dressing:* In a mixing bowl, stir together mayonnaise, chives, cilantro, and sherry. Sprinkle and stir in curry powder to taste.

2. *Plump raisins:* In a small saucepan, gently heat sherry. Add raisins and set aside until plumped, about 15 minutes. Drain.

3. *Mix and arrange salad:* In a mixing bowl, toss crabmeat, celery, chopped apple and pear, chopped pecans, and plumped raisins with enough dressing to coat well. Arrange lettuce leaves on individual serving plates and mound crab salad in centers. Garnish with fans of apple slices, pecan halves, and cilantro sprigs.

MAKES 4 GENEROUS SERVINGS

Seafood Louis

Although it looks like simplicity itself, and is very easy to prepare, this classic, remarkably refreshing seafood salad is exceptionally satisfying—due in large part to the rich and vibrantly seasoned dressing.

LOUIS DRESSING
1 cup mayonnaise
½ cup crème fraîche
¼ cup bottled chili sauce
2 tablespoons finely chopped fresh
  chives
1 to 2 tablespoons prepared horseradish
4 to 6 drops Tabasco sauce

SALAD
6 cups coarsely shredded romaine
  lettuce leaves, chilled in the
  refrigerator
6 cups coarsely shredded iceberg lettuce
  leaves, chilled in the refrigerator
¾ pound cooked bay shrimp
¾ pound cooked crabmeat, flaked coarse
  and picked clean of shell and cartilage
4 hard-boiled eggs, quartered lengthwise
4 firm ripe Roma tomatoes, cored and
  quartered lengthwise
1 firm ripe Haas avocado
1 lemon, cut into 4 wedges

1. *Make dressing:* In a mixing bowl, stir ingredients together, adding horseradish and Tabasco to taste. Cover and refrigerate.

2. *Arrange salad:* Toss together lettuces and pile into large individual serving bowls. Spread out bay shrimp on one side of each salad, flaked crabmeat on the other side. Place eggs and tomatoes around edge of each bowl. Halve, pit, and peel avocado and cut lengthwise into thin slices; arrange slices on top of each salad. Serve, accompanied by lemon wedges, and pass dressing alongside.

MAKES 4 GENEROUS SERVINGS

Sautéed Bay Scallop Salad with Roasted Peppers and Pine Nuts on Baby Spinach

In this seafood variation on the popular hot spinach salad, sweet little bay scallops are sautéed and finished with a sauce that becomes the dressing for the salad leaves.

12 cups thoroughly washed and
   stemmed baby spinach leaves
¼ cup vegetable oil
2 large shallots, chopped fine
1½ pounds small sea scallops, trimmed
   of any connective tissue
1 large red bell pepper, roasted, peeled,
   stemmed, seeded (see Index), and cut
   into ¼-by-1- to 2-inch strips, juices
   reserved

1 large yellow bell pepper, roasted,
   peeled, stemmed, seeded (see Index),
   and cut into ¼-by-1- to 2-inch strips,
   juices reserved
¼ cup balsamic vinegar
¼ cup olive oil
½ cup pine nuts, toasted (see Index)
2 tablespoons finely shredded fresh basil

    1. *Prepare salad leaves:* On individual serving plates, arrange the spinach leaves in beds.

    2. *Cook scallops:* In a large skillet, heat vegetable oil over moderate to high heat. Add shallots and sauté about 30 seconds. Add scallops and sauté, stirring briskly, just until done, about 1 minute.

    3. *Deglaze pan and serve salad:* Add peppers, vinegar, and olive oil to skillet. Stir and scrape about 30 seconds. Spoon scallops, peppers, and juices over spinach. Garnish with pine nuts and basil. Serve immediately.

MAKES 4 GENEROUS SERVINGS

Chilled Poached Lobster Salad with Salmon Caviar and Lemon Dill Cream Dressing

Fittingly for lobster, simple elegance reigns in this salad—a perfect main course for a special warm-weather luncheon or light supper. Lobster tails alone are becoming increasingly available in upscale fish markets and supermarket seafood departments. The salmon roe caviar—a lavish-seeming touch—is relatively inexpensive and widely available at gourmet delis.

POACHED LOBSTER
1 bottle dry white wine
1 large onion, sliced thick
1 large carrot, sliced thick
1 large celery stalk, sliced thick
2 large sprigs parsley
2 sprigs fresh thyme
2 small bay leaves
¼ teaspoon salt
¼ teaspoon whole peppercorns
4 lobster tails in the shell

LEMON DILL CREAM DRESSING
3 tablespoons lemon juice
1½ tablespoons finely chopped fresh dill
½ teaspoon salt
⅛ teaspoon white pepper
¾ cup heavy cream

SALAD
12 cups whole small Bibb lettuce leaves
1 pound thin baby haricots verts (French green beans), boiled until tender-crisp and cooled
12 medium-sized field mushrooms, sliced thin
¼ cup salmon roe caviar
¼ cup finely chopped fresh chives
2 tablespoons finely shredded fresh basil

1. *Poach and cool lobster:* In a saucepan, bring wine, onion, carrot, celery, parsley, thyme, bay leaves, salt, and peppercorns to a boil; reduce heat to low and simmer, covered, 15 minutes. Raise heat to moderate and add lobster tails; simmer briskly until lobster is done, 7 to 10 minutes. Remove from pan, let come to room temperature, and chill in refrigerator.

2. *Shell and slice lobster:* With the tip of a small, sharp knife, carefully cut through shells lengthwise along underside of each lobster tail. With your thumbs, carefully pry apart shells and peel away from meat. Cut each tail crosswise into 5 medallions.

3. *Make dressing:* Just before serving, stir together lemon juice, dill, salt, and pepper. Let stand 2 to 3 minutes, then, whisking continuously, pour in cream in a steady stream.

4. *Assemble salad:* Arrange salad leaves attractively on individual serving plates. In a mixing bowl, toss together haricots verts and mushrooms with just enough dressing to coat; arrange in center of each plate. Array lobster medallions, overlapping slightly, on top of haricots and mushrooms. Drizzle dressing over lobster, and top with caviar. Scatter chives and basil over salads.

MAKES 4 GENEROUS SERVINGS

California-Style Grilled Lobster Salad with Golden Tomatoes, Roasted Peppers, Avocado, and Sun-Dried Tomato Pesto Vinaigrette

Some of the now-familiar trademark ingredients of contemporary California cuisine—baby lettuces, sun-dried tomatoes, roasted peppers, pine nuts—join together in this elegant salad.

SUN-DRIED TOMATO PESTO VINAIGRETTE

6 tablespoons olive oil
6 tablespoons packed drained sun-dried tomatoes
¼ cup lemon juice
2 tablespoons pine nuts, toasted (see Index)
2 tablespoons Parmesan cheese
8 large fresh basil leaves
1 small garlic clove

GRILLED LOBSTER

3 cups water
1 cup dry white wine
1 large onion, sliced thick
1 large carrot, sliced thick
1 large celery stalk, sliced thick
2 large sprigs parsley
2 sprigs cilantro
2 small bay leaves
½ teaspoon whole black peppercorns
4 lobster tails in the shell
3 tablespoons olive oil
1 tablespoon lemon juice
Salt
White pepper

SALAD

12 cups mixed baby salad leaves (see Index)
12 whole baby golden or red plum tomatoes, or 4 firm ripe Roma tomatoes, quartered
1 red bell pepper, roasted, stemmed, seeded (see Index), and torn into long, thin strips
1 yellow bell pepper, roasted, stemmed, seeded (see Index), and torn into long, thin strips
1 green bell pepper, roasted, stemmed, seeded (see Index), and torn into long, thin strips
1 large firm ripe Haas avocado
2 tablespoons pine nuts, toasted (see Index)
1 tablespoon finely chopped fresh chives
1 tablespoon finely shredded fresh basil

1. *Make dressing:* Put all vinaigrette ingredients into a food processor with the metal blade. Pulse the machine several times until mixture is coarsely chopped; then process continuously, stopping 2 or 3 times to scrape down sides of bowl, until dressing is smooth. Set aside.

2. *Prepare lobster:* In a saucepan, bring water, wine, onion, carrot, celery, parsley, cilantro, bay leaves, and black peppercorns to a boil; reduce heat, cover, and simmer 15 minutes. Raise heat and, when liquid boils again, add lobster tails and cook 3 minutes. Drain and rinse lobster tails under cold running water until cool enough to handle. With the tip of a small, sharp knife, carefully cut through shells lengthwise along underside of each lobster tail. With your thumbs, carefully pry apart shells and peel away from meat. Cut each tail crosswise into 5 medallions. In a bowl, toss medallions with olive oil and lemon juice.

3. *Grill lobster:* Preheat grill or broiler until very hot. Sprinkle lobster medallions with salt and white pepper and grill just until cooked through, 1 to 1½ minutes per side.

4. *Arrange salad:* Arrange salad leaves and tomatoes on individual serving plates. Strew pepper strips on top. Place grilled lobster medallions on each salad. Halve, pit, and peel avocado and cut lengthwise into thin slices; place around lobster medallions. Spoon dressing over lobster and other salad ingredients. Garnish with pine nuts, chives, and basil.

MAKES 4 GENEROUS SERVINGS

Southwestern Seviche on a Bed of Baby Greens

"Cooked" by the acidity of its citrus marinade, the fresh raw seafood in this salad turns firm in texture and opaque in color without losing any of its pristine tenderness or refreshing ocean flavor. Favorite modern southwestern embellishments maintain a link to the dish's Latin American origins.

When preparing fresh chilies, be aware that their volatile oils can cause burning if they come into contact with any sensitive surfaces—cuts, abrasions, eyes, nose, etc. Handle the chilies carefully, using kitchen gloves if necessary, and wash your hands thoroughly with soap and water when finished.

SOUTHWESTERN SEVICHE

¾ pound fresh sea scallops, trimmed of tough connective tissue, each scallop sliced into 2 equal rounds
½ pound fresh swordfish fillet, skinned if necessary, cut into ¾-inch chunks
½ pound fresh salmon fillet, skinned if necessary, cut into ¾-inch chunks
1 large red onion, chopped coarse
2 red serrano chilies, stemmed, seeded, and chopped fine
1 jalapeño chili, stemmed, seeded, and chopped fine
½ cup fresh lime juice
¼ cup fresh lemon juice
¼ cup fresh orange juice
1 teaspoon salt
½ teaspoon white pepper

SALAD

2 firm ripe Haas avocados
½ pound jicama, peeled and cut into ¼-by-1-inch strips
1 large navel orange, segmented, membranes removed, fruit cut into ¾-inch chunks
1 red bell pepper, stemmed, seeded, and cut into ½-inch squares
1 green bell pepper, stemmed, seeded, and cut into ½-inch squares
¼ cup finely chopped cilantro
¾ cup olive oil
12 baby radicchio leaves
12 baby oak leaf lettuce leaves
12 baby Bibb lettuce leaves
12 Belgian endive leaves
4 nasturtium blossoms

1. *Marinate seafood:* In a glass, ceramic, or other nonreactive mixing bowl, combine the scallops, swordfish, salmon, onion, chilies, citrus juices, salt, and pepper. Cover and refrigerate for 3 to 4 hours, stirring occasionally, until seafood is opaque and firm. Drain off and discard excess liquid.

2. *Combine seviche with other salad ingredients:* Shortly before serving, halve, pit, and peel avocados and cut into ¾-inch chunks. Toss gently with seafood, jicama, orange, bell peppers, cilantro, and just enough oil to coat.

3. *Arrange and serve salad:* On individual serving plates, arrange salad leaves in concentric rosette patterns. Mount seviche mixture in centers. Garnish with nasturtium blossoms.

MAKES 4 GENEROUS SERVINGS

2

POULTRY SALADS

Country-Fried Chicken Salad with Blue Cheese, Apples, Pecans,
and Cider Honey Vinaigrette

Chinese Almond Chicken Salad
with Sesame Ginger Dressing on a Bed of Crisp Rice Sticks

Grilled Mandarin Chicken Salad with Tangerine Vinaigrette and Baby Greens

Grilled Chicken and Goat Cheese Salad
with Sun-Dried Tomatoes and Basil Pesto Vinaigrette

Chicken Fajitas Salad on a Bed of Crisp Greens with Cilantro Lime Vinaigrette

Grilled Chicken Tostada with Blue Corn Tortilla Strips,
Black Beans, and Chile Colorado Vinaigrette

Grilled Chicken Cobb with Creamy Dijon Mustard Vinaigrette

Chicken Salad à la Waldorf

Classic Turkey Cobb with Red Wine–Mustard Vinaigrette

Turkey Paillard with Sweet Corn, Grilled Tomatoes, and Onions
on a Bed of Bitter Greens with Balsamic Vinaigrette

Herb-Poached Rolled Turkey Breast with Winter Vegetables
and Grainy Dijon Mustard Vinaigrette

Curried Turkey Salad in Pineapple Boats

Smoked Turkey Salad with Provolone,
Peppers, Tart Apples, Walnuts, and Basil Lemon Mayonnaise

Grilled Duck Breast Salad with Wilted Red Cabbage,
Roquefort, Bacon, and Warm Golden Raisin Vinaigrette

Grilled Duck Breast Salad with Baby Spinach, Hazelnuts,
and Raspberry Vinaigrette

Grilled Duck Breast Salad with Avocado, Tropical Fruit Salsa, and Baby Greens

Grilled Duck Sausage Salad with Peppers and Onions, Pistachio Nuts,
Mixed Baby Greens, and Raspberry Vinaigrette

Country-Fried Chicken Salad with Blue Cheese, Apples, Pecans, and Cider Honey Vinaigrette

Like an old-fashioned picnic, this salad combines a satisfying variety of down-home foods. You can, in fact, bring it along on a picnic. Just fry up the chicken in advance, cut it up, and pack the strips carefully—along with the other ingredients—in separate containers, to be dressed and tossed just before serving.

COUNTRY-FRIED CHICKEN
4 boneless skinless chicken
  breast halves
1 cup milk
½ cup all-purpose flour
½ cup yellow cornmeal
1 tablespoon finely chopped
  fresh parsley
1 teaspoon mild paprika
½ teaspoon salt
¼ teaspoon black pepper
2 eggs, lightly beaten
Vegetable oil for frying

CIDER HONEY
VINAIGRETTE
3 tablespoons cider vinegar
2 tablespoons honey, at room
  temperature
1 tablespoon lemon juice
1 tablespoon coarse-grained
  mustard
½ teaspoon salt
¼ teaspoon white pepper
¼ cup walnut oil
½ cup vegetable oil

SALAD
3 cups torn romaine lettuce
  leaves
3 cups torn oak leaf lettuce
  leaves
3 cups torn butter lettuce leaves
3 cups torn curly endive leaves
2 medium-sized tart eating
  apples, peeled, cored, cut into
  ¾-inch chunks, and tossed
  with juice of ½ lemon
½ pound good-quality blue
  cheese, crumbled
1 cup shelled pecan halves,
  toasted (see Index)
2 tablespoons finely chopped
  fresh chives

1. *Bread chicken:* Put chicken breast halves between 2 sheets of waxed paper and pound with kitchen mallet or heel of your hand until uniformly ½ to ¾ inch thick. Soak in milk for 30 minutes; drain. Dredge halves in ¼ cup of flour to coat. In a shallow bowl, stir together remaining flour, cornmeal, parsley, paprika, salt, and pepper. Dredge chicken in egg, then immediately in cornmeal mixture to coat evenly. On work surface, gently tap breast 8 times in crosshatch pattern with dull edge of large chef's knife to secure coating. Gently dredge breasts in egg again, coat with more cornmeal mixture, and tap once more. Set aside ½ hour for coating to set.

2. *Fry chicken:* Heat ½ inch of oil in large, heavy skillet over moderate to high heat. Fry chicken until golden brown and cooked through, 4 to 5 minutes per side. Remove to paper towels to drain.

3. *Make dressing:* While chicken is frying, stir together vinegar, honey, lemon juice, mustard, salt, and pepper. Whisking continuously, slowly stir in walnut and vegetable oils. Set aside.

4. *Assemble salad:* Toss salad leaves with just enough dressing to coat. Arrange a bed of leaves on each of four large serving plates or in shallow bowls. Scatter apples, blue cheese, and pecans on top. Cut chicken breast halves crosswise into ½-inch-wide slices, arrange on top of salads, and drizzle with remaining dressing. Garnish with chives.

MAKES 4 GENEROUS SERVINGS

Chinese Almond Chicken Salad with Sesame Ginger Dressing on a Bed of Crisp Rice Sticks

This attractive interpretation of a classic Chinese chicken salad is a great way to use up leftover chicken.

SESAME GINGER DRESSING
¼ cup rice vinegar
¼ cup soy sauce
2 tablespoons finely grated fresh
   gingerroot
2 teaspoons sugar
1 teaspoon dry mustard
½ cup peanut oil
2 tablespoons sesame oil

SALAD
3 cups boneless skinless cooked chicken
   meat, torn into ¼- to ½-inch-by-1- to
   2-inch shreds
Vegetable oil for deep frying
4 ounces dry thin rice-stick noodles
6 cups thinly shredded napa cabbage
   leaves
6 cups thinly shredded romaine lettuce
   leaves
1 cup blanched almonds, toasted (see
   Index)
1 cup water-packed canned mandarin
   orange segments, drained well
¼ cup black sesame seeds or toasted (see
   Index) white sesame seeds
¼ cup finely chopped cilantro
2 scallions, sliced thin crosswise
4 large cilantro sprigs

1. *Make dressing:* In a container with a tight-fitting lid, stir together vinegar, soy sauce, ginger, sugar, and mustard until well combined. Add peanut and sesame oils, cover and shake well.

2. *Marinate chicken:* Put cooked chicken in a large mixing bowl, add dressing, and toss well. Cover and marinate in refrigerator for 30 minutes to 1 hour.

3. *Fry noodles:* Shortly before serving, heat 2 to 3 inches of vegetable oil in a wok or heavy skillet until very hot. A small handful at a time, drop noodles carefully into hot oil and submerge with a wire skimmer or slotted spoon: they will expand and puff in a matter of seconds. Remove immediately to drain on paper towels and repeat with remaining noodles. Arrange noodles, breaking them up as necessary, on a platter or individual plates.

4. *Toss and serve salad:* Drain off dressing from chicken and reserve. In mixing bowl, toss marinated chicken and remaining ingredients except cilantro sprigs with enough dressing to coat. Mound on top of rice noodles. Garnish with cilantro sprigs.

MAKES 4 GENEROUS SERVINGS

Grilled Mandarin Chicken Salad
with Tangerine Vinaigrette and Baby Greens

This is an elegant, formalized variation on Chinese chicken salad.

TANGERINE VINAIGRETTE
¼ cup tangerine juice
2 tablespoons lemon juice
2 teaspoons creamy Dijon-style
  mustard
½ teaspoon salt
½ teaspoon black pepper
½ cup peanut oil
6 tablespoons sesame oil

SALAD
4 large boneless skinless chicken
  breast halves
3 tablespoons tangerine juice
1 tablespoon sesame oil
1 tablespoon peanut oil
Peanut oil for deep frying
4 packaged square Chinese
  wonton skins, cut into ¼-inch-
  wide strips
Salt
White pepper
12 cups mixed baby salad leaves
  (see Index)
12 large dried shiitake
  mushrooms, soaked in warm
  water for 15 minutes, stems
  removed, caps cut into ¼-
  inch-wide slices

24 ears canned or bottled baby
  corn
24 fresh litchis, peeled, pitted,
  and halved, *or* 16 canned
  litchis, rinsed and halved
1 cup cashews, toasted (see
  Index)
2 tablespoons finely chopped
  fresh chives
2 tablespoons coarsely chopped
  cilantro

1. *Make dressing:* In a mixing bowl, stir together tangerine juice, lemon juice, mustard, salt, and pepper. Whisking continuously, slowly pour in peanut and sesame oils until blended.

2. *Marinate chicken:* In a shallow dish, coat chicken with tangerine juice and sesame and peanut oils. Marinate at room temperature for 30 minutes.

3. *Fry wonton strips:* While chicken is marinating, in a heavy skillet or wok heat 1 to 2 inches of oil until very hot. Add wonton strips—in 2 or 3 batches if necessary, to prevent overcrowding—and fry until crisp and golden, 2 to 3 minutes. Remove with slotted spoon or wire skimmer and drain on paper towels.

4. *Grill chicken:* Preheat grill or broiler until very hot. Season chicken with salt and pepper and grill until cooked through and golden brown, 4 to 5 minutes per side.

5. *Toss and arrange salad:* While chicken cooks, in a large mixing bowl toss salad leaves with enough dressing to coat. Arrange leaves attractively in beds on individual serving plates. Arrange wonton strips, shiitakes, baby corn, litchis, and cashews on top. When chicken is done, cut each breast crosswise into ½-inch-wide slices and place on top of salads. Drizzle lightly with remaining dressing. Garnish with chives and cilantro.

MAKES 4 GENEROUS SERVINGS

Grilled Chicken and Goat Cheese Salad with Sun-Dried Tomatoes and Basil Pesto Vinaigrette

Here's a quintessential California nouvelle-style salad. In inspiration, it owes a debt to Michael McCarty's famous lunchtime salad served at his Santa Monica restaurant, but I've chosen to use skinless chicken breasts and have added the signature Golden State flourishes of sun-dried tomatoes and pine nuts.

BASIL PESTO VINAIGRETTE
⅔ cup olive oil
½ cup packed fresh basil leaves
2 tablespoons balsamic vinegar
2 tablespoons lemon juice
2 tablespoons pine nuts, toasted (see Index)
2 tablespoons Parmesan cheese
1 small garlic clove

GRILLED CHICKEN
2 tablespoons lemon juice
2 tablespoons lime juice
2 tablespoons olive oil
4 large boneless skinless chicken breast halves
6 ounces fresh creamy goat cheese, chilled
Salt
White pepper

SALAD
12 cups mixed baby salad leaves
1 large red bell pepper, roasted, stemmed, seeded (see Index), and torn into long thin strips
1 large yellow bell pepper, roasted, stemmed, seeded (see Index), and torn into long thin strips
½ cup packed drained sun-dried tomato pieces, cut into ½-inch pieces
½ cup pine nuts, toasted (see Index)
2 tablespoons finely chopped fresh chives
2 tablespoons finely shredded fresh basil

1. *Make dressing:* Put all dressing ingredients into a food processor with the metal blade. Pulse the machine several times until mixture is coarsely chopped; then process continuously, stopping 2 or 3 times to scrape down sides of bowl, until dressing is smooth. Set aside.

2. *Marinate chicken:* In a shallow bowl, stir together lemon juice, lime juice, and olive oil. Turn chicken in bowl to coat; marinate 15 minutes at room temperature.

3. *Stuff and grill chicken:* Preheat grill or broiler until very hot. Meanwhile, with a small, sharp knife, cut a deep horizontal pocket in the thickest side of each chicken breast. Stuff the pockets with goat cheese, patting breasts to distribute it evenly and pinching opening closed. Season chicken with salt and pepper and grill until cooked through and golden brown, 4 to 5 minutes per side, basting chicken with marinade before turning.

4. *Arrange salad:* While chicken grills, arrange salad leaves in attractive patterns on individual serving plates. When chicken is done, cut each breast crosswise into ½-inch slices and place in center of plate. Garnish with peppers, sun-dried tomatoes, and pine nuts. Spoon dressing over chicken and other salad ingredients. Garnish with chives and basil.

MAKES 4 GENEROUS SERVINGS

Chicken Fajitas Salad on a Bed of Crisp Greens with Cilantro Lime Vinaigrette

A favorite southwestern main course, normally eaten wrapped in tortillas, gets the salad treatment here. Feel free to serve warmed flour or corn tortillas on the side, if you like.

CILANTRO LIME VINAIGRETTE
¾ cup olive oil
¼ cup lime juice
1 teaspoon creamy Dijon-style mustard
2 tablespoons finely chopped cilantro
½ teaspoon salt
½ teaspoon white pepper
½ teaspoon sugar

SALAD
1½ pounds boneless skinless chicken breasts, cut crosswise into ½-inch-wide strips
2 fresh green Anaheim (long mild) chilies, halved, stemmed, seeded, and cut crosswise into ¼-inch-wide strips
2 large scallions, halved lengthwise and cut into 1-inch pieces
1 red bell pepper, halved, stemmed, seeded, and cut crosswise into ¼-inch-wide strips
1 green bell pepper, halved, stemmed, seeded, and cut crosswise into ¼-inch-wide strips
1 large red onion, cut into ¼-inch-thick slices, rings separated
¼ cup lemon juice

1 tablespoon dried oregano
1 teaspoon salt
1 teaspoon black pepper
¼ cup olive oil
1 large ripe Haas avocado
1 tablespoon lime juice
1 tablespoon finely chopped cilantro
Salt and pepper to taste
12 cups shredded romaine lettuce leaves, chilled in the refrigerator
¼ pound Monterey Jack cheese, shredded
¼ pound sharp cheddar cheese, shredded
½ cup sour cream
2 cups packaged blue or yellow corn tortilla chips
½ cup pitted black olives, cut in halves
4 cilantro sprigs

1. *Make dressing:* Put all ingredients in a container with a tight-fitting lid. Shake well. Set aside.

2. *Marinate fajitas:* In a mixing bowl, toss chicken, chilies, scallions, bell peppers, and onion with lemon juice, oregano, salt, pepper, and half the olive oil. Cover and marinate at room temperature 15 to 30 minutes.

3. *Prepare avocado:* Halve, pit, and peel avocado; mash with lime juice, chopped cilantro, and salt and pepper to taste. Set aside.

4. *Cook fajitas:* In a large, heavy skillet, heat remaining olive oil over high heat. Lift fajitas mixture from marinade and spread evenly in skillet; sear until undersides are well browned, 1 to 2 minutes. Stir and sauté until chicken is done, 3 to 5 minutes more. Pour some of marinade in skillet and quickly stir and scrape to dissolve pan deposits.

5. *Dress and assemble salad:* Toss romaine with enough dressing to coat, and arrange in beds on individual serving plates. Scatter fajitas over romaine. Sprinkle with cheeses. Garnish with dollops of sour cream and mashed avocado, tortilla chips, olives, and cilantro sprigs. Pass any remaining dressing on the side.

MAKES 4 GENEROUS SERVINGS

Grilled Chicken Tostada with Blue Corn Tortilla Strips, Black Beans, and Chile Colorado Vinaigrette

This contemporized version of a classic features chicken breasts marinated in citrus juices and grilled, then accompanied by some of the hallmarks of the modern southwestern kitchen.

CHILE COLORADO VINAIGRETTE

4 long dried red Anaheim chilies
¾ cup olive oil
2 tablespoons balsamic vinegar
2 tablespoons lemon juice
½ tablespoon dried oregano
¼ teaspoon salt
¼ teaspoon white pepper

GRILLED CHICKEN AND BLUE CORN TORTILLA STRIPS

2 tablespoons lemon juice
2 tablespoons lime juice
2 tablespoons orange juice
2 tablespoons olive oil
1 tablespoon dried oregano
1 teaspoon dried rosemary
4 large boneless skinless chicken breast halves
Vegetable oil for deep frying
4 blue or gold corn tortillas, cut into ¼-inch-wide strips
Salt
White pepper

SALAD

1 large firm ripe Haas avocado
2 tablespoons lime juice
2 tablespoons canned chopped mild green chilies
2 tablespoons finely chopped cilantro
6 cups coarsely torn romaine lettuce leaves, chilled in refrigerator
2 cups coarsely torn radicchio leaves
2 cups coarsely torn oak leaf lettuce leaves
2 cups coarsely torn Bibb lettuce leaves
2 cups cooked, rinsed, and drained whole black beans (canned or home-cooked)
1 cup cooked corn kernels
6 firm ripe Roma tomatoes, cored and chopped coarse
½ cup sour cream
3 ounces Monterey Jack cheese, shredded
3 ounces sharp cheddar cheese, shredded
Cilantro sprigs

1. *Make dressing:* Preheat oven to 400°F. Put chilies on a baking sheet and toast in oven just until slightly darkened in color, 3 to 4 minutes; take care not to burn them. When cool enough to handle, split open, stem, and seed. Tear chilies into rough pieces and put with other dressing ingredients in a processor with the metal blade. Process until smoothly blended, stopping 2 or 3 times to scrape down bowl. Set aside.

2. *Marinate chicken:* In a shallow bowl, stir together lemon, lime, and orange juices, olive oil, oregano, and rosemary. Turn chicken in bowl to coat; cover and marinate in refrigerator 1 hour, turning chicken 2 or 3 times.

3. *Fry tortillas:* While chicken is marinating, heat 1 to 2 inches oil in a heavy skillet or wok until very hot. Add tortilla strips and fry until crisp, about 1 minute. Remove with wire skimmer and drain on paper towels.

4. *Grill chicken:* Preheat grill or broiler until very hot. Season chicken with salt and pepper, and grill until cooked through and golden brown, 4 to 5 minutes per side, basting chicken with marinade before turning.

5. *Arrange salad:* While chicken is grilling, halve, pit, and peel avocado; mash coarsely with lime juice, chilies, and cilantro. Set aside. In a mixing bowl, toss together romaine, radicchio, oak leaf, and Bibb lettuces with just enough dressing to coat; arrange in beds on individual serving plates. Spread black beans in center of each plate. Scatter half of tortilla strips on top of beans. When chicken is done, cut each breast crosswise into ½-inch-wide strips and place on center of salad; drizzle with more dressing. Scatter corn and tomatoes around chicken. Top with remaining tortilla strips, dollops of avocado and sour cream, shredded cheese, and cilantro sprigs.

MAKES 4 GENEROUS SERVINGS

Grilled Chicken Cobb with
Creamy Dijon Mustard Vinaigrette

When you're hosting fairly conservative salad eaters but want to offer them something different, try this contemporary version of a classic.

CREAMY DIJON MUSTARD VINAIGRETTE
See Index

GRILLED CHICKEN
2 tablespoons balsamic vinegar
2 tablespoons lemon juice
2 tablespoons olive oil
1 teaspoon dried rosemary
4 large boneless skinless chicken breast halves
Salt
Black pepper

SALAD
8 cups coarsely chopped romaine lettuce leaves
2 cups coarsely shredded radicchio leaves
2 cups thinly sliced Belgian endive leaves
8 slices streaky smoked bacon, fried crisp and crumbled coarse
4 hard-boiled eggs, halved, yolks and whites separated, and chopped coarse
6 ounces Roquefort or Stilton cheese, crumbled
2 medium-sized firm ripe Haas avocados
24 miniature golden or red plum tomatoes, or cherry tomatoes, halved
2 tablespoons finely shredded fresh basil

1. *Make dressing:* See Index for Creamy Dijon Mustard Vinaigrette.
2. *Marinate chicken:* In a shallow bowl, stir together vinegar, lemon juice, olive oil, and rosemary. Turn chicken in bowl to coat; marinate 15 to 30 minutes.

3. *Grill chicken:* Preheat grill or broiler until very hot. Season chicken with salt and pepper and grill until cooked through and golden brown, 4 to 5 minutes per side, basting with marinade before turning.

4. *Arrange and serve salad:* In a mixing bowl, toss together romaine, radicchio, and endive with just enough dressing to coat; arrange on individual serving plates. In neat rows or concentric circles on top of lettuce, arrange bacon, egg, and Roquefort or Stilton. Cut each chicken breast crosswise into ½-inch-wide slices and arrange on top of each salad. Halve, pit, and peel avocados and cut lengthwise into thin slices; arrange beside and slightly overlapping chicken; intersperse with tomato halves. Drizzle more dressing on top and garnish with basil.

MAKES 4 GENEROUS SERVINGS

Chicken Salad à la Waldorf

The classic late-nineteenth-century recipe first served by chef Oscar Tschirky at the Waldorf in New York inspired this quickly prepared luncheon salad featuring leftover chicken.

2 cups coarsely chopped cooked chicken meat

4 large firm apples, 3 peeled, cored, and chopped into ¾-inch pieces, 1 cored, sliced thin, and tossed with 2 tablespoons lemon juice

3 celery stalks, stringed and cut crosswise into ¼-inch-thick slices

1 cup coarsely chopped walnuts, toasted (see Index)

2 tablespoons finely chopped fresh chives

2 tablespoons finely chopped Italian parsley

2 tablespoons lemon juice

1 tablespoon honey

1 cup mayonnaise

8 cups shredded romaine lettuce leaves, chilled in refrigerator

Fresh parsley sprigs

1. *Mix salad:* In a mixing bowl, toss together chicken, chopped apples, celery, walnuts, chives, and parsley. Drizzle in lemon juice and honey, then mix in enough mayonnaise to coat well.

2. *Arrange salad:* Arrange romaine in a bed on a platter or large individual serving plates. Mound salad mixture in center. Garnish with apple slices and parsley sprigs.

MAKES 4 GENEROUS SERVINGS

Classic Turkey Cobb with
Red Wine–Mustard Vinaigrette

A definitive version of a classic combination. You can, if you like, toss all the ingredients together in a large serving bowl, but I prefer to present individual servings with the ingredients neatly arranged, for each diner to dress and mix to taste.

RED WINE–MUSTARD VINAIGRETTE

¼ cup red-wine vinegar

2 tablespoons coarse-grained Dijon-style mustard

½ teaspoon salt

½ teaspoon black pepper

½ teaspoon sugar

¾ cup olive oil

SALAD

12 cups coarsely chopped romaine lettuce leaves

3 cups coarsely chopped cooked turkey breast

8 slices streaky smoked bacon, fried crisp and crumbled coarse

6 firm ripe Roma tomatoes, stemmed, seeded, and chopped coarse

4 hard-boiled eggs, halved, yolks and whites separated, and chopped fine

6 ounces blue cheese, crumbled

2 medium-sized firm ripe Haas avocados

1. *Make dressing:* In a mixing bowl, stir together vinegar, mustard, salt, pepper, and sugar. Whisking continuously, slowly pour in oil until blended. Set aside.

2. *Arrange and serve salad:* In large individual salad bowls, arrange beds of romaine. In neat rows on top of lettuce, arrange turkey, bacon, tomato, egg, and blue cheese, leaving room for avocado. Just before serving, halve, pit, and peel avocados and cut into ½-inch chunks; arrange on top of salads. Pass dressing on the side.

MAKES 4 GENEROUS SERVINGS

Turkey Paillard with Sweet Corn, Grilled Tomatoes, and Onions on a Bed of Bitter Greens with Balsamic Vinaigrette

With the growing popularity of turkey as an everyday—rather than only special-occasion—main course, supermarket meat sections are beginning to carry such intriguing options as steaks cut from the breast meat. Sometimes you'll find big slices, in the style of a French paillard of veal; at the very least, you'll find smaller breast slices. Both work well in this satisfying salad.

BALSAMIC VINAIGRETTE
¼ cup balsamic vinegar
1 tablespoon creamy Dijon-style
   mustard
¼ teaspoon salt
¼ teaspoon white pepper
¾ cup olive oil

TURKEY PAILLARD
2 tablespoons lemon juice
2 tablespoons olive oil
1 tablespoon finely chopped fresh chives
1½ pounds turkey breast, cut into large
   ½-inch-thick slices
Salt
Black pepper

SALAD
4 large Roma tomatoes, halved
   lengthwise
1 large Maui, Vidalia, Walla Walla, or
   sweet red onion, cut into ½-inch-thick
   slices
2 tablespoons olive oil
Salt
Black pepper
4 cups coarsely torn curly endive leaves
4 cups coarsely torn radicchio leaves
4 cups coarsely torn rocket leaves
1½ cups cooked sweet corn kernels
2 tablespoons finely shredded fresh basil

1. *Make dressing:* In a mixing bowl, stir together vinegar, mustard, salt, and pepper. Whisking continuously, very slowly pour in oil until blended.

2. *Marinate turkey:* In a shallow bowl, stir together lemon juice, olive oil, and chives. Turn the turkey slices in bowl to coat; marinate 15 to 30 minutes at room temperature.

3. *Grill turkey:* Preheat grill or broiler until very hot. Season turkey with salt and pepper and grill just until cooked through and golden, 3 to 4 minutes per side, basting with marinade before turning.

4. *Grill vegetables:* When turkey is cooking on second side, brush tomato halves and onion slices with olive oil and sprinkle with salt and pepper. Grill until nicely seared, 30 seconds to 1 minute per side.

5. *Arrange salad:* In a mixing bowl, toss salad leaves with enough dressing to coat. Arrange on individual serving plates. Scatter corn kernels over each salad. Drape turkey slices over salads and arrange tomato halves and onion rings around them. Drizzle with dressing and garnish with basil.

MAKES 4 GENEROUS SERVINGS

Herb-Poached Rolled Turkey Breast
with Winter Vegetables
and Grainy Dijon Mustard Vinaigrette

This homey treatment of butcher shop–bought turkey breast slices and humble vegetables gets an elegant edge from the herbs that flavor the turkey—which is rolled up, poached, chilled, and sliced—and from the baby salad leaves that serve as the salad's foundation.

HERB-POACHED ROLLED TURKEY BREAST WITH WINTER VEGETABLES

1 tablespoon olive oil
1 tablespoon lemon juice
½ tablespoon dried oregano
½ tablespoon dried rosemary
½ tablespoon dried thyme
½ tablespoon dried savory
1½ pounds turkey breast, cut into slices ½ inch thick and about 4 inches across
1 quart chicken broth
1 bay leaf
6 whole black peppercorns

1 medium-sized carrot, cut crosswise into ¼- to ½-inch-thick slices
1 medium-sized celery stalk, cut crosswise into ¼- to ½-inch-thick slices
1 medium-sized leek, white part only, thoroughly washed and cut crosswise into ¼- to ½-inch-thick slices
1 medium-sized zucchini, halved lengthwise and cut crosswise into ¼- to ½-inch-thick slices

GRAINY DIJON MUSTARD VINAIGRETTE
See Index

SALAD
12 cups mixed baby salad leaves (see Index)
2 tablespoons finely chopped fresh chives
2 tablespoons finely chopped fresh Italian parsley

1. *Cook turkey and vegetables:* In a mixing bowl, stir together olive oil, lemon juice, and dried herbs. Spread herb mixture evenly on one side of each turkey breast slice. Starting at longest edge of each slice, tightly roll it up, enclosing herb mixture like the filling of a jelly roll. With kitchen string, tie each roll securely at each end and at 1- to 2-inch intervals. In a saucepan, bring broth to a boil with bay leaf and peppercorns. Reduce heat to bare simmer, add turkey rolls, and poach until done, 10 to 15 minutes. Remove rolls from pan and set aside. One kind at a time, cook vegetables in simmering broth just until tender-crisp; remove with a slotted spoon and set aside.

2. *Chill turkey and vegetables:* Put turkey rolls and vegetables in a bowl or dish and pour over them just enough broth to cover. Refrigerate until well chilled, 2 to 3 hours.

3. *Make dressing:* See Index for Grainy Dijon Mustard Vinaigrette.

4. *Slice turkey and toss salad:* Remove turkey and vegetables from refrigerator. Drain well. With a small, sharp knife, cut strings from turkey rolls and cut rolls crosswise into ¼- to ½-inch-thick slices. In a mixing bowl, toss turkey, poached vegetables, and salad leaves with enough dressing to coat. Mound on individual salad plates and garnish with chives and parsley.

MAKES 4 GENEROUS SERVINGS

Curried Turkey Salad in Pineapple Boats

Let's face it: sometimes you *have* to go to extremes to bring excitement to leftovers. That's why, cornball as it may seem, pineapple boats are a perfect vehicle for the pickings from that holiday turkey.

CURRIED HERB MAYONNAISE
See Index

SALAD
2 medium-sized ripe pineapples, with
    leaves, cut in halves lengthwise
3 cups coarsely chopped cooked turkey
2 medium-sized celery stalks, sliced thin
    crosswise
1 red bell pepper, halved, stemmed,
    seeded, and cut into ¼-inch dice
½ cup raisins
½ cup pine nuts, toasted (see Index)
Cilantro sprigs

1. *Make dressing:* See Index for Curried Herb Mayonnaise.
2. *Make pineapple boats:* With a small, sharp knife and a keen-edge spoon, remove and discard the pineapple cores and then hollow out and save the fruit, leaving shells about ½ inch thick. Coarsely chop the pineapple fruit.
3. *Mix and serve salad:* In a mixing bowl, toss chopped pineapple, turkey, celery, pepper, raisins, and pine nuts with enough dressing to coat. Mound into pineapple boats and garnish with cilantro sprigs.

MAKES 4 GENEROUS SERVINGS

Smoked Turkey Salad with Provolone, Peppers, Tart Apples, Walnuts, and Basil Lemon Mayonnaise

I tend to think of this as a real autumn or winter salad, full of rich, sharp flavors and textures to liven up a dreary day. Smoked turkey is readily available at good deli counters.

BASIL LEMON MAYONNAISE
1 cup mayonnaise
½ cup packed fresh basil leaves
1 tablespoon lemon juice
1 teaspoon finely grated lemon zest

SALAD
1½ pounds thinly sliced smoked turkey, cut into ½-inch-wide strips
½ pound thinly sliced provolone cheese, cut into ¼-inch-wide strips
1 large tart green eating apple, cored and cut into ½-inch chunks
1 red bell pepper, quartered, stemmed, seeded, and cut crosswise into ¼-inch-wide strips
½ cup broken walnut pieces, toasted (see Index)
24 medium-sized oak leaf lettuce leaves
24 Belgian endive leaves
2 tablespoons finely chopped fresh chives
2 tablespoons finely chopped fresh Italian parsley

1. *Make dressing:* Put mayonnaise, basil, lemon juice, and zest in a processor with the metal blade. Pulse machine until basil is well processed into mayonnaise, with only small flecks of leaf showing in the pale-green sauce.

2. *Mix and arrange salad:* In a mixing bowl, toss turkey, provolone, apple, pepper, and walnuts with enough dressing to coat. On a platter or individual serving plates, arrange a bed of oak leaf lettuce; on top, arrange endive leaves like spokes on a wheel. Mound turkey mixture in center; garnish with dollops of dressing, chives, and parsley.

MAKES 4 GENEROUS SERVINGS

Grilled Duck Breast Salad with Wilted Red Cabbage, Roquefort, Bacon, and Warm Golden Raisin Vinaigrette

The inspiration for this dish comes from the classic French appetizer salad of red cabbage with hot bacon vinaigrette that I first tasted at Saint-Estèphe, my friend John Sedlar's legendary restaurant in Manhattan Beach, California.

GRILLED DUCK
1 tablespoon finely chopped fresh sage
2 teaspoons salt
2 teaspoons black pepper
4 boned duck breasts, about 6 ounces each

WILTED RED CABBAGE AND ROQUEFORT
¼ cup kosher salt
10 cups finely shredded red cabbage
6 ounces Roquefort cheese, crumbled

WARM GOLDEN RAISIN VINAIGRETTE AND GARNISHES
4 thick slices bacon, cut crosswise into ½-inch-wide pieces
2 slices good-quality white bread, crusts trimmed, bread cut into 8 small triangles each
¼ cup balsamic vinegar
½ cup vegetable oil
¼ cup walnut oil
½ cup seedless golden raisins
1½ tablespoons creamy Dijon-style mustard
Salt and pepper to taste
2 tablespoons finely chopped fresh chives

1. *Marinate duck:* In a shallow dish, toss together sage, salt, and pepper, and rub mixture well into duck breasts. Leave to marinate for about 30 minutes.

2. *Wilt cabbage:* Bring a large pot of water to a boil. Add kosher salt and then plunge cabbage into water. After 30 seconds, drain and let cabbage cool in strainer. In a large mixing bowl, toss cabbage with Roquefort and set aside.

3. *Prepare croutons and dressing:* In a medium-sized skillet, cook bacon over moderate heat until golden, about 4 minutes. Remove bacon from skillet and set aside; add bread triangles, turn quickly in bacon fat, sauté until crisp and golden, 3 to 4 minutes more, and set aside. Pour off any remaining fat from skillet. Add vinegar, quickly stir and scrape to deglaze, and stir in vegetable and walnut oils, raisins, Dijon mustard, and salt and pepper to taste. Remove from heat and set aside.

4. *Grill duck:* Preheat grill or broiler until very hot. Grill duck until medium-rare to medium, 3 to 4 minutes per side.

5. *Assemble salad:* Arrange cabbage mixture in beds on individual serving plates. Scatter bacon on top and spoon warm dressing with raisins over each plate to coat. Cut each duck breast crosswise at a 45-degree angle into ¼-inch-thick slices and array on top of cabbage. Place croutons around duck. Garnish with chives.

MAKES 4 GENEROUS SERVINGS

Grilled Duck Breast Salad with Baby Spinach, Hazelnuts, and Raspberry Vinaigrette

This salad version of a nouvelle cuisine–inspired combination of ingredients is so long-established that it's virtually a classic.

RASPBERRY VINAIGRETTE
¼ cup raspberry vinegar
2 teaspoons creamy Dijon-style mustard
½ teaspoon salt
½ teaspoon white pepper
½ teaspoon sugar
¾ cup olive oil

SALAD
4 boned duck breasts, about 6 ounces each
Salt
Black pepper
12 cups stemmed and washed baby spinach leaves
¾ cup coarsely chopped hazelnuts, toasted (see Index)
1 cup fresh raspberries
2 tablespoons finely chopped fresh chives

1. *Make dressing:* In a bowl, stir together vinegar, mustard, salt, pepper, and sugar. Whisking continuously, slowly pour in olive oil until blended. Set aside.

2. *Grill duck:* Preheat grill or broiler until very hot. Season duck with salt and pepper and grill until medium-rare to medium, 3 to 4 minutes per side.

3. *Assemble salad:* Toss spinach and hazelnuts with enough dressing to coat. Arrange leaves in beds on individual serving plates. Cut each duck breast crosswise at a 45-degree angle into ¼-inch-thick slices and array on top of leaves. Distribute raspberries decoratively over spinach and on top of duck. Garnish with chives.

MAKES 4 GENEROUS SERVINGS

Grilled Duck Breast Salad with Avocado, Tropical Fruit Salsa, and Baby Greens

The rich, meaty quality of duck gets a wonderful spark from the colorful, zesty salsa that dresses this salad.

TROPICAL FRUIT SALSA
½ cup finely chopped fresh pineapple
½ cup finely chopped fresh mango
½ cup finely chopped fresh kiwifruit
¾ cup olive oil
¼ cup lime juice
2 tablespoons orange juice
1 teaspoon finely grated lime zest
1 teaspoon finely grated orange zest
½ teaspoon salt
½ teaspoon white pepper
2 small jalapeño chilies, roasted, stemmed, peeled, seeded (see Index), and chopped fine

SALAD
4 boned duck breasts, about 6 ounces each
Salt
Black pepper
12 cups mixed baby salad leaves (see Index)
1 large firm ripe Haas avocado
2 tablespoons finely chopped cilantro

1. *Make salsa:* In a bowl, stir together all ingredients. Set aside.

2. *Grill duck:* Preheat grill or broiler until very hot. Season duck with salt and pepper and grill until medium-rare to medium, 3 to 4 minutes per side.

3. *Assemble salad:* Toss salad leaves with enough liquid from salsa to coat. Arrange leaves in an attractive pattern on individual serving plates. Cut each duck breast crosswise at a 45-degree angle into ¼-inch-thick slices and array on top of leaves. Halve, pit, and peel avocado and cut lengthwise into thin slices; arrange slices around duck. Spoon solids from salsa over duck and avocado. Garnish with cilantro.

MAKES 4 GENEROUS SERVINGS

Grilled Duck Sausage Salad with Peppers and Onions, Pistachio Nuts, Mixed Baby Greens, and Raspberry Vinaigrette

Many upscale butcher shops and meat departments today carry outstanding freshly made duck sausages, which have a delectable savoriness highlighted to advantage in this salad. The grilled peppers and onions that accompany it are a nod to the traditional Italian accompaniments to grilled sausages.

RASPBERRY VINAIGRETTE
See Index

SALAD
4 large fresh duck sausages
1 large red bell pepper, halved, stemmed, seeded, and cut into 8 wedges
1 large yellow bell pepper, halved, stemmed, seeded, and cut into 8 wedges
1 large green bell pepper, halved, stemmed, seeded, and cut into 8 wedges
1 large Vidalia, Maui, Walla Walla, or sweet red onion, cut into ½-inch-thick slices

3 tablespoons olive oil
Salt
Black pepper
12 cups mixed baby salad leaves (see Index)
4 large ripe Roma tomatoes, cored and quartered
6 tablespoons shelled pistachio nuts
2 tablespoons finely chopped fresh chives

1. *Make dressing:* See Index for Raspberry Vinaigrette.

2. *Cook sausages:* Put sausages in a saucepan of cold water. Bring to a boil over moderate heat. Meanwhile, preheat grill or broiler until very hot. Drain sausages and grill until seared golden brown, 3 to 4 minutes per side.

3. *Grill vegetables:* When sausages are cooking on second side, brush pepper wedges and onion slices with olive oil and sprinkle with salt and pepper. Grill until nicely seared, 30 seconds to 1 minute per side.

4. *Arrange salad:* In a mixing bowl, toss salad leaves with just enough dressing to coat. Arrange in beds on individual serving plates. Cut each sausage diagonally into ½-inch-thick slices and array across each salad. Place grilled vegetables and quartered tomatoes around sausages. Scatter pistachios over sausage slices. Drizzle with more dressing and garnish with chives.

MAKES 4 GENEROUS SERVINGS

3

MEAT SALADS

Grilled Sirloin with Spicy Caesar Salad

Provençal Beef Salad with Country Greens and Anchovy Shallot Vinaigrette

Classic Beef Taco Salad with Salsa Vinaigrette

Grilled Steak Salad with Beefsteak Tomatoes, Grilled Potatoes
and Onions, Bitter Greens, and Creamy Blue Cheese Dressing

Red Flannel Hash Salad with Mustard Chili Mayonnaise

Grilled Veal Saddle Salad with Sun-Dried Tomatoes, Peppers,
Baby Greens, and Basil Pesto Vinaigrette

Grilled Veal Sausage and Potato Salad with German Mustard
and Caraway Seed Vinaigrette

Vitello Tonnato Salad on a Bed of Rocket and Radicchio
with Tuna-Anchovy-Caper Mayonnaise

Greek Country-Style Lamb Salad with Oregano Mint Vinaigrette

Tandoori-Style Lamb Tenderloin with Spinach,
Mixed Raita Dressing, and Crisp Papadums

Grilled Lamb Tenderloin Salad with Baby Lettuces and Raspberry Vinaigrette

Italian Chef's Salad with Gorgonzola Vinaigrette

Classic Chopped Salad

Grilled Pork Tenderloin Salad with Grilled Apples, Bitter Greens,
Pecans, and Cider Honey Vinaigrette

Thai-Style Grilled Pork Salad with Red Onions, Crushed Peanuts,
Baby Spinach, and Lime Mint Vinaigrette

Chinese Barbecued Pork Salad with Crisp Vegetables and Hoisin Vinaigrette

Cajun Andouille Sausage Salad with Baby Greens and Spicy Pecan Vinaigrette

Grilled Sirloin with Spicy Caesar Salad

This robust version of the classic salad includes a slightly spicier Caesar dressing to complement the grilled steak.

SPICY CAESAR DRESSING
4 anchovy fillets
2 medium-sized garlic cloves, crushed
3 tablespoons lemon juice
1 tablespoon Worcestershire sauce
½ teaspoon dry mustard
¼ teaspoon Tabasco sauce
1 large egg
½ cup olive oil

GRILLED SIRLOIN
1½ pounds sirloin steak
¼ cup Worcestershire sauce
Salt
Black pepper

SALAD
14 cups coarsely torn romaine lettuce leaves, chilled in the refrigerator
2 cups garlic herb croutons (see Index)
6 tablespoons freshly grated Parmesan cheese
2 tablespoons finely chopped fresh chives

1. *Make dressing:* Bring a small saucepan of water to a boil. Meanwhile, in a shallow mixing bowl, mash together anchovies and garlic with a fork or the back of a spoon until smooth. Stir in lemon juice, Worcestershire, mustard, and Tabasco. Drop egg into boiling water; boil 50 seconds, rinse under cold running water, and break into mixing bowl. Whisking constantly, slowly pour in oil until blended. Set aside.

2. *Marinate and grill steak:* In a bowl, coat steak with Worcestershire and marinate about 15 minutes. Meanwhile, heat grill or broiler until very hot. Season steak with salt and pepper and grill until done medium-rare, 2½ to 3 minutes per side.

3. *Arrange salad:* Toss romaine, croutons, and Parmesan with enough dressing to coat well. Arrange in beds on individual plates. Cut steak into ¼-inch-thick slices and drape over salads. Garnish with chives.

MAKES 4 GENEROUS SERVINGS

Provençal Beef Salad with Country Greens and Anchovy Shallot Vinaigrette

Traditional country greens and a tangy anchovy-spiked dressing from the south of France highlight the flavor of cold roast beef in this robust yet elegant combination. If you don't have a leftover roast on hand, by all means use good-quality rare roast beef from your local deli counter. If you can't get the leaves suggested here, substitute such dark green lettuces as oak leaf or small Boston or Bibb leaves.

ANCHOVY SHALLOT VINAIGRETTE

6 anchovy fillets, rinsed and patted dry
3 tablespoons red-wine vinegar
1 tablespoon lemon juice
2 small shallots, chopped fine
1 tablespoon finely chopped Italian parsley
¾ cup olive oil

SALAD

3 cups watercress, coarsely torn into bite-sized sprigs
3 cups small rocket leaves, left whole
3 cups curly endive leaves, coarsely torn into bite-sized pieces
3 cups radicchio leaves, coarsely torn into bite-sized pieces

1½ pounds leftover rare roast beef, cut into long, thin slices
¾ pound firm ripe tomatoes, stemmed and cut into ¾-inch chunks
¾ cup Niçoise-style marinated black olives, pitted
2 tablespoons finely chopped fresh chives

1. *Prepare dressing:* In a mixing bowl, use a fork to mash anchovies with vinegar and lemon juice until smooth. Stir in shallots and parsley. Whisking continuously, very slowly pour in olive oil until blended. Set aside.

2. *Arrange and serve salad:* Toss together salad leaves with just enough dressing to coat and arrange in a bed on a serving platter or large individual plates. Drape beef across greens in a decorative pattern, interspersed with tomato chunks and olives. Drizzle more dressing on top and sprinkle with chives.

MAKES 4 GENEROUS SERVINGS

Classic Beef Taco Salad with Salsa Vinaigrette

I ate my first taco salad back in the mid-1960s at the restaurant in the old May Company department store in downtown Los Angeles. It seemed very exotic then, and for a whole summer it was my lunchtime staple. Though such salads are fairly common now, none I've eaten out since has equaled that first one. Here's my re-creation of that landmark experience.

SALSA VINAIGRETTE

2 medium-sized firm ripe tomatoes, stemmed, halved, seeded, and diced fine
3 tablespoons lime juice
2 tablespoons good-quality red-wine vinegar
2 tablespoons canned chopped mild green chilies
1 tablespoon finely chopped cilantro
¾ teaspoon sugar
½ teaspoon salt
½ teaspoon white pepper
¾ cup olive oil

SALAD

2 tablespoons vegetable oil
2 medium-sized garlic cloves, chopped fine
1 medium-sized onion, chopped fine
1½ pounds lean ground beef
2 tablespoons good-quality chili powder
2 tablespoons lime juice
3 firm ripe Haas avocados
6 cups coarsely torn iceberg lettuce leaves
6 cups coarsely torn romaine lettuce leaves
2 cups drained canned kidney beans
2 cups coarsely crushed packaged corn chips
1 cup pitted black olives, sliced
½ pound sharp cheddar cheese, shredded
16 large whole romaine lettuce leaves
½ cup sour cream
1 lime or lemon, cut into wedges
1 cup whole packaged corn chips
4 large sprigs Italian parsley or cilantro

1. *Make dressing:* In a mixing bowl, stir together tomatoes, lime juice, vinegar, chilies, cilantro, sugar, salt, and pepper. Stir in olive oil and set aside.

2. *Cook taco beef:* In a large skillet, heat oil over moderate to high heat. Add garlic and onion and sauté until translucent, 1 to 2 minutes. Add beef and sauté, stirring constantly, until well browned, 5 to 7 minutes. Sprinkle on chili powder and lime juice and sauté, stirring, 1 minute more.

3. *Toss and assemble salad:* As soon as beef is done, halve, pit, and peel avocados; cut 2 into ½- to ¾-inch chunks, the third into long, thin slices. In a large mixing bowl, toss avocado chunks with torn lettuces, kidney beans, crushed corn chips, olives, about two-thirds of the cheese, half of the beef, and enough dressing to coat. Arrange whole romaine leaves around sides of large deep individual salad bowls or plates. Mound salad inside. Scatter remaining beef on top. Garnish with remaining cheese, dollops of sour cream, avocado slices, lime or lemon wedges, whole corn chips, and sprigs of parsley or cilantro.

MAKES 4 GENEROUS SERVINGS

Grilled Steak Salad with Beefsteak Tomatoes, Grilled Potatoes and Onions, Bitter Greens, and Creamy Blue Cheese Dressing

Not even the heartiest of eaters could deny that this salad is a meal in itself.

CREAMY BLUE CHEESE DRESSING
½ cup mayonnaise
¼ cup sour cream
½ teaspoon black pepper
¼ pound blue cheese, crumbled coarse

GRILLED SIRLOIN, POTATOES,
AND ONIONS
12 medium-sized red-skinned new
  potatoes
1½ pounds sirloin steak
Salt
Black pepper
1 large Vidalia, Maui, or Walla Walla
  onion, cut into ½-inch-thick slices
2 tablespoons olive oil

SALAD
4 cups coarsely torn radicchio leaves
4 cups coarsely torn rocket leaves
4 cups coarsely torn curly endive leaves
2 medium-sized firm ripe beefsteak
  tomatoes *or* 8 firm ripe Roma
  tomatoes, cored and cut into ½-inch-
  thick slices
2 cups garlic croutons (see Index)
2 tablespoons finely chopped fresh
  chives

1. *Make dressing:* Put mayonnaise, sour cream, pepper, and half of cheese in a food processor with the metal blade. Process until smoothly blended. Transfer to a mixing bowl and fold in remaining cheese. Cover and refrigerate.

2. *Grill steak and vegetables:* Put potatoes in a saucepan, cover with cold water, bring to a boil, and simmer just until they are easily pierced by the tip of a small, sharp knife; drain well and rinse under cold running water until cool enough to handle; cut into

½-inch-thick slices. Meanwhile, heat grill or broiler until very hot. Season steak with salt and pepper and grill until done medium-rare, 2½ to 3 minutes per side. As soon as meat is turned over, brush potatoes and onion with oil, season with salt and pepper, and grill until golden, about 1 minute per side.

3. *Arrange salad:* Toss salad leaves together and arrange in beds on individual plates. Arrange tomato slices in middle of each plate. Drizzle dressing over tomatoes and greens. Cut steak into ¼-inch-thick slices and drape over tomatoes; drizzle with a little more dressing. Arrange potatoes, onions, and croutons around steak. Garnish with chives.

MAKES 4 GENEROUS SERVINGS

Red Flannel Hash Salad with Mustard Chili Mayonnaise

This variation on a favorite old New England breakfast is a delicious way to utilize leftover corned beef, roast beef, or ham. Since it's a luncheon dish here, I've added chopped pickled cucumbers and let the mayonnaise dressing take the place of eggs.

MUSTARD CHILI MAYONNAISE
¾ cup mayonnaise
2 tablespoons coarse-grained Dijon-style mustard
2 tablespoons bottled chili sauce
1 teaspoon Worcestershire sauce
½ teaspoon Tabasco sauce

SALAD
1 pound leftover corned beef, roast beef, or ham, cut into ½-inch cubes
2 medium-sized beets, boiled until tender-crisp, peeled, and cut into ½-inch cubes
2 medium-sized baking potatoes, peeled, quartered, boiled until just tender, cooled, and cut into ½-inch cubes
2 large pickled dill cucumbers, cut into ½-inch cubes
1 large green bell pepper, stemmed, seeded, and cut into ½-inch squares
1 medium-sized red onion, chopped fine
¼ cup finely chopped Italian parsley
16 large Bibb lettuce leaves
12 firm ripe cherry tomatoes, halved
2 tablespoons finely chopped fresh chives

1. *Make dressing:* In a mixing bowl, stir together all ingredients. Set aside.

2. *Mix and arrange salad:* In a mixing bowl, toss cubed meat, beets, potatoes, pickles, bell pepper, onion, and parsley with enough dressing to coat well. Arrange lettuce leaves on a large platter or individual serving plates. Mound salad in center. Garnish with cherry tomato halves and chives.

MAKES 4 GENEROUS SERVINGS

Grilled Veal Saddle Salad with Sun-Dried Tomatoes, Peppers, Baby Greens, and Basil Pesto Vinaigrette

Fresh, lively flavors, textures, and colors complement the sweet, mild flavor and tender texture of good-quality veal in this California-style salad.

BASIL PESTO VINAIGRETTE
See Index

GRILLED VEAL SADDLE
2 tablespoons lemon juice
2 tablespoons olive oil
1 tablespoon coarse-grained Dijon-style mustard
4 boneless veal saddles, about 6 ounces each
Salt
White pepper

SALAD
12 cups mixed baby salad leaves (see Index)
1 large red bell pepper, halved, stemmed, seeded, and cut crosswise into ¼-inch-wide thin strips
1 large yellow bell pepper, halved, stemmed, seeded, and cut crosswise into ¼-inch-wide thin strips
½ cup packed drained sun-dried tomato pieces, cut into ¼-inch-wide strips
½ cup pine nuts, toasted (see Index)
2 tablespoons finely chopped fresh chives
2 tablespoons finely shredded fresh basil

1. *Make dressing:* See Index for Basil Pesto Vinaigrette.

2. *Marinate veal:* In a shallow bowl, stir together lemon juice, olive oil, and mustard. Turn veal in bowl to coat; marinate 15 to 30 minutes at room temperature.

3. *Grill veal:* Preheat grill or broiler until very hot. Season veal with salt and pepper and grill until done medium, about 3 minutes per side.

4. *Arrange salad:* Arrange salad leaves in attractive patterns on individual serving plates. Cut veal crosswise into ¼-inch slices and place in center of plates. Garnish with peppers, sun-dried tomato strips, and pine nuts. Spoon dressing over veal and other salad ingredients. Garnish with chives and basil.

MAKES 4 GENEROUS SERVINGS

Grilled Veal Sausage and Potato Salad with German Mustard and Caraway Seed Vinaigrette

This robust salad reminds me of the kind of luncheon dish you might be served in a German country inn. You'll find fresh white veal sausages at well-stocked butcher or deli counters.

GERMAN MUSTARD AND
CARAWAY VINAIGRETTE
¼ cup red-wine vinegar
2 tablespoons German-style brown
    mustard
1 tablespoon whole caraway seeds
½ teaspoon salt
½ teaspoon white pepper
½ teaspoon sugar
¾ cup vegetable oil

GRILLED VEAL SAUSAGE AND
POTATO SALAD
16 small red-skinned new potatoes
4 fresh bratwurst (white veal sausages)
2 tablespoons finely chopped fresh
    chives
2 tablespoons finely chopped fresh
    Italian parsley

SALAD
16 whole Bibb lettuce leaves
4 cups watercress sprigs
4 cups finely shredded red cabbage
    leaves
1 large red bell pepper, roasted, peeled,
    seeded (see Index), and torn into thin
    strips
1 large green bell pepper, roasted,
    peeled, seeded (see Index), and torn
    into thin strips
4 large firm ripe Roma tomatoes, cored
    and quartered

1. *Make dressing:* In a mixing bowl, stir together vinegar, mustard, caraway seeds, salt, pepper, and sugar. Whisking continuously, slowly pour in oil until blended. Set aside.

2. *Boil potatoes and sausages:* In 2 separate saucepans, cover potatoes and sausages with cold water. Bring water to a boil. Drain sausages and set aside. Reduce heat under potatoes and simmer briskly until tender enough to be pierced by the tip of a small, sharp knife. Drain well.

3. *Marinate potatoes:* Holding hot potatoes one at a time in a folded kitchen towel, cut—skins and all—into ¼-inch-thick slices; put in a mixing bowl. Pour enough dressing over them to coat generously; add chives and parsley, toss gently, and set aside.

4. *Grill sausages:* Preheat grill or broiler until very hot. Grill sausages until seared golden brown, 3 to 4 minutes per side.

5. *Arrange salad:* Place Bibb leaves on individual serving plates. Spread a bed of watercress and cabbage on top of lettuce in center of each plate; drizzle with dressing. Arrange marinated potato slices on top of cabbage. Cut each sausage diagonally into ½-inch-thick slices and array on top of potatoes. Place pepper strips and tomato quarters around sausage.

MAKES 4 GENEROUS SERVINGS

Vitello Tonnato Salad on a Bed of Rocket and Radicchio with Tuna-Anchovy-Caper Mayonnaise

While this Italian-inspired salad is great with leftover roast veal, it also works wonderfully with turkey breast. You could also prepare it with freshly grilled veal saddle or turkey breast (see Index).

TUNA-ANCHOVY-CAPER
MAYONNAISE
1 (6½-ounce) can tuna in oil, drained
  and flaked coarse
4 anchovy fillets, drained
2 medium-sized garlic cloves, peeled
  and chopped coarse
½ cup mayonnaise
1 tablespoon drained capers
1 tablespoon finely chopped Italian
  parsley
1 tablespoon lemon juice
1 tablespoon olive oil
¼ teaspoon black pepper

SALAD
6 cups coarsely torn radicchio leaves
6 cups coarsely torn rocket leaves
1½ pounds cold roast veal, cut into ¼-
  inch-thick slices
6 firm ripe Roma tomatoes, cored and
  quartered
2 tablespoons finely chopped chives
2 tablespoons finely chopped Italian
  parsley
1½ tablespoons drained capers

1. *Make dressing:* Put all ingredients in a food processor with the metal blade. Pulse 2 or 3 times, then process until smoothly pureed, stopping several times to scrape down the bowl. Cover and refrigerate.

2. *Arrange salad:* Toss together radicchio and rocket and arrange in beds on individual serving plates. Drape veal slices on top and arrange tomato wedges around veal. Spoon dressing over veal and garnish with chives, parsley, and capers.

MAKES 4 GENEROUS SERVINGS

Greek Country-Style Lamb Salad
with Oregano Mint Vinaigrette

This main-course variation on the classic Greek *horiatiki* salad is one of the best ways I know to serve leftover cold lamb—be it from a roast leg of lamb, lamb chops, or whatever.

OREGANO MINT
VINAIGRETTE
¼ cup red-wine vinegar
¼ teaspoon salt
1 tablespoon finely chopped
   fresh mint leaves
1 teaspoon dried oregano
½ teaspoon dry mustard
¼ teaspoon black pepper
¾ cup olive oil

SALAD
1½ pounds leftover cooked lamb,
   well trimmed, cut into slices
   about ¼ inch thick, 1 inch
   wide, and 2 to 3 inches long
½ pound feta cheese, cut into ½-
   inch cubes
½ pound firm ripe tomatoes,
   stemmed and cut into ¾-inch
   chunks
1 large cucumber, peeled,
   halved lengthwise, seeded,
   and cut crosswise into ¼-inch-
   thick slices

1 large red onion, sliced thin
¾ cup Greek-style marinated
   black olives, pitted
8 cups thinly sliced romaine
   lettuce leaves, chilled in the
   refrigerator
½ cup pine nuts, toasted (see
   Index)

1. *Make dressing:* In a mixing bowl, stir together vinegar and salt until salt dissolves; then stir in herbs, mustard, and pepper. Very slowly pour in olive oil, whisking continuously until blended. Set aside.

2. *Toss and serve salad:* In a large mixing bowl, toss salad ingredients—except for romaine and pine nuts—with just enough dressing to coat. Toss romaine with enough of remaining dressing to coat and arrange in bed on a serving platter or large individual plates. Mound salad on top and garnish with pine nuts.

MAKES 4 GENEROUS SERVINGS

Tandoori-Style Lamb Tenderloin with Spinach, Mixed Raita Dressing, and Crisp Papadums

The huge beehive-shaped tandoori ovens of Indian cuisine produce an intense, dry heat that turns foods cooked in it appealingly seared on the outside, succulent and moist within. While no one I know has a home tandoori oven, it is possible to approximate the results by using an Indian-style spiced yogurt marinade and grilling or broiling food—the technique employed in this recipe. The lamb turns out intriguingly spiced—but by no means fiery in taste.

A yogurt dressing derived from a popular Indian side dish completes the spinach-based salad, which is garnished with crisp papadums—lentil wafers available packaged in the ethnic food section of good-sized supermarkets.

TANDOORI-STYLE LAMB TENDERLOIN
½ cup plain low-fat yogurt
1 tablespoon finely grated gingerroot
1 tablespoon finely grated onion
1 teaspoon ground cardamom
1 teaspoon cayenne pepper
1 teaspoon ground coriander
1 teaspoon ground cumin
½ teaspoon ground turmeric
1 small garlic clove, chopped fine
1 small hot fresh green chili, stemmed, seeded, and chopped fine
4 lamb tenderloins, 4 to 6 ounces each
Salt and pepper to taste

MIXED RAITA DRESSING
¾ cup plain low-fat yogurt
¼ cup lemon juice
1 tablespoon finely chopped fresh mint
1 tablespoon finely chopped cilantro
½ teaspoon salt
½ teaspoon white pepper
1 pickling cucumber, unpeeled and cut into ¼-inch pieces
1 firm ripe Roma tomato, cored, halved, seeded, and cut into ¼-inch pieces
1 large shallot, chopped fine

SALAD
Vegetable oil for deep frying
4 spiced papadum wafers
12 cups finely shredded thoroughly washed spinach leaves
1 medium-sized red onion, sliced thin
¼ cup mixed fruit chutney
1 lemon, cut into 4 wedges
Cilantro sprigs

1. *Marinate lamb:* In a mixing bowl, stir together yogurt, ginger, onion, spices, garlic, and chili. Turn lamb in mixture to coat; cover and refrigerate 1 hour.

2. *Make dressing:* In a mixing bowl, stir together all ingredients. Cover and refrigerate.

3. *Fry papadums:* In a heavy skillet or large wok, heat 1 to 2 inches of vegetable oil until very hot. Fry papadum wafers one at a time, using the back of a wire skimmer to keep it fully submerged; the instant the wafer expands completely, within just a few seconds, remove and drain on paper towels.

4. *Grill lamb:* Heat grill or broiler until very hot. Season lamb with salt and pepper and grill until done medium-rare, 2½ to 3 minutes per side.

5. *Arrange salad:* Arrange spinach in beds on individual serving plates. Cut tenderloins into ¼-inch-thick slices and drape over spinach. Spoon dressing over lamb and spinach. Strew sliced onions over salad. Place a dollop of chutney on lamb. Carefully break each papadum into 4 wedges and place around sides of salad. Place a lemon wedge on each plate and garnish with cilantro sprigs.

MAKES 4 GENEROUS SERVINGS

Grilled Lamb Tenderloin Salad with Baby Lettuces and Raspberry Vinaigrette

The sweet sharpness of a raspberry vinaigrette plays up the distinctive flavor and tender meatiness of the lamb in this elegant, simple salad.

RASPBERRY VINAIGRETTE
See Index

GRILLED LAMB TENDERLOIN
2 tablespoons raspberry vinegar
2 tablespoons olive oil
4 lamb tenderloins, 4 to 6 ounces each
Salt
Black pepper

SALAD
12 cups mixed baby salad leaves (see Index)
1 large red bell pepper, roasted, peeled, seeded (see Index), and torn into thin strips
1 large yellow bell pepper, roasted, peeled, seeded (see Index), and torn into thin strips
6 tablespoons pine nuts, toasted (see Index)
2 tablespoons finely chopped fresh chives
2 tablespoons finely shredded fresh basil

1. *Make dressing:* See Index for Raspberry Vinaigrette.

2. *Marinate and grill lamb:* In a shallow bowl, stir together vinegar and oil and turn lamb tenderloins to coat; marinate about 15 minutes at room temperature. Meanwhile, heat grill or broiler until very hot. Season lamb with salt and pepper and grill until done medium-rare, 2½ to 3 minutes per side.

3. *Arrange salad:* Toss salad leaves with enough dressing to coat. Arrange in beds on individual plates. Cut tenderloins into ¼-inch-thick slices and drape over salads. Strew peppers around lamb. Garnish with pine nuts, chives, and basil.

MAKES 4 GENEROUS SERVINGS

Italian Chef's Salad with Gorgonzola Vinaigrette

This is a lively, tangy version of the classic salad.

GORGONZOLA VINAIGRETTE
¼ cup balsamic vinegar
2 tablespoons creamy Dijon-style mustard
1 tablespoon dried oregano
½ teaspoon salt
½ teaspoon black pepper
½ teaspoon sugar
¾ cup olive oil
6 tablespoons crumbled Gorgonzola cheese

SALAD
6 cups coarsely chopped romaine lettuce leaves
6 cups coarsely chopped iceberg lettuce leaves
¼ pound thinly sliced prosciutto, cut into ½-inch-wide strips
¼ pound thinly sliced cooked Italian ham, cut into ½-inch-wide strips
¼ pound thinly sliced bresaola (air-cured beef), cut into ½-inch-wide strips
¼ pound thinly sliced provolone cheese, cut into ½-inch-wide strips
16 cherry tomatoes, stemmed and halved
12 small whole pepperoncini (Italian pickled peppers), drained
½ cup Italian-style marinated black olives

1. *Make dressing:* In a mixing bowl, stir together vinegar, mustard, oregano, salt, pepper, and sugar. Whisking continuously, slowly pour in oil until blended. Stir in Gorgonzola. Set aside.

2. *Arrange and serve salad:* Toss together romaine and iceberg and arrange in beds in large individual salad bowls. Toss together meat and cheese strips and scatter on top of lettuce. Distribute tomatoes, pepperoncini, and olives on top. Pass dressing on the side.

MAKES 4 GENEROUS SERVINGS

Classic Chopped Salad

A standby of so many favorite neighborhood Italian restaurants, this salad is traditionally made in a large wooden bowl, all the ingredients chopped together with a *mezzaluna*— a crescent moon-shaped chopping tool. But, assuming that most homes aren't equipped with that device, the instructions here—which take only a little bit longer—call for the individual ingredients to be cut up separately and tossed together just before serving.

ITALIAN VINAIGRETTE
1 small garlic clove, crushed
¼ teaspoon salt
3 tablespoons red-wine vinegar
1 teaspoon creamy Dijon-style mustard
½ teaspoon dried basil
½ teaspoon dried oregano
¼ teaspoon black pepper
¾ cup olive oil

SALAD
6 cups coarsely chopped romaine lettuce leaves
6 cups coarsely chopped iceberg lettuce leaves
1 cup canned garbanzo beans, drained and chopped coarse
½ cup pitted black olives, chopped coarse
¾ pound thinly sliced Genoa salami, chopped coarse
½ pound mozzarella cheese, shredded coarse
¼ pound provolone cheese, sliced thin and chopped coarse
4 small firm ripe Roma tomatoes, stemmed and chopped coarse
8 pepperoncini (Italian pickled peppers), stemmed and chopped coarse (optional)

1. *Make dressing:* In a shallow bowl, use a fork or the back of a spoon to mash together the garlic and salt until smooth. Stir in vinegar, mustard, basil, oregano, and pepper. Slowly add oil in a thin stream, whisking continuously, until smoothly blended. Set aside.

2. *Combine and toss salad:* In a large mixing bowl, toss together all salad ingredients. Transfer to individual serving bowls and pass dressing; or toss salad in mixing bowl with enough dressing to coat.

MAKES 4 GENEROUS SERVINGS

Grilled Pork Tenderloin Salad with Grilled Apples, Bitter Greens, Pecans, and Cider Honey Vinaigrette

Stylish though this salad is, it nevertheless evokes a sort of down-home quality with its combination of pork, apples, pecans, and peppers—all joined by a sweet-sharp vinaigrette.

CIDER HONEY VINAIGRETTE
See Index

GRILLED PORK TENDERLOIN AND
GRILLED APPLES
2 tablespoons cider vinegar
2 tablespoons honey
2 tablespoons vegetable oil
4 pork tenderloins, 4 to 6 ounces each
Salt
Black pepper
2 tart green apples, cored and cut
   vertically into ½-inch-thick slices

SALAD
4 cups coarsely torn radicchio leaves
4 cups watercress sprigs
4 cups coarsely torn curly endive leaves
¾ cup pecan halves, toasted (see Index)
1 large red bell pepper, halved,
   stemmed, seeded, and cut into ¼-inch-
   wide strips
2 tablespoons finely chopped fresh
   chives
2 tablespoons finely shredded fresh basil

1. *Make dressing:* See Index for Cider Honey Vinaigrette.

2. *Marinate and grill pork and apples:* In a shallow bowl, stir together cider vinegar, honey, and oil and turn pork tenderloins to coat; marinate about 15 minutes at room temperature. Meanwhile, heat grill or broiler until very hot. Season pork with salt

and pepper and grill until done medium, 3 to 4 minutes per side. After turning pork over, dip apple slices in marinade and grill until golden, about 1 minute per side.

3. *Arrange salad:* Toss salad greens, pecans, and pepper strips with enough dressing to coat. Arrange in beds on individual plates. Cut pork tenderloins into $\frac{1}{4}$-inch-thick slices and drape over salads. Place grilled apple rings around and slightly overlapping pork. Garnish with chives and basil.

MAKES 4 GENEROUS SERVINGS

Thai-Style Grilled Pork Salad with Red Onions, Crushed Peanuts, Baby Spinach, and Lime Mint Vinaigrette

Sharp, satisfying flavors characterize this slightly westernized version of a traditional Thai salad. If you like, ask your butcher to flatten the pork fillets for you.

LIME MINT VINAIGRETTE
3 tablespoons lime juice
2 tablespoons finely chopped fresh mint
1 tablespoon rice vinegar
½ tablespoon soy sauce
½ cup peanut oil
2 tablespoons sesame oil

THAI-STYLE GRILLED PORK
2 tablespoons soy sauce
2 tablespoons lime juice
1 tablespoon honey
1 tablespoon peanut oil
1 tablespoon sesame oil
1 garlic clove, chopped very fine
1 small hot green chili, sliced thin
1½ pounds pork fillets, pounded to a ¼-inch thickness

SALAD
12 cups thoroughly washed baby spinach leaves
1 medium-sized red onion, sliced very thin
½ cup coarsely crushed peanuts, toasted (see Index)
2 tablespoons finely chopped cilantro

1. *Make dressing:* Put all ingredients in a container with a tight-fitting lid. Shake well. Set aside.

2. *Marinate pork:* In a shallow dish, stir together soy, lime juice, honey, peanut and sesame oils, garlic, and chili. Turn pork in dish to coat. Cover and marinate in refrigerator 1 to 2 hours.

3. *Grill pork:* Heat grill or broiler until very hot. Grill pork until well seared and cooked through, 2 to 3 minutes per side.

4. *Arrange salad:* Toss spinach leaves, onion, and peanuts with enough dressing to coat. Arrange in beds on individual plates. Drape pork on top; drizzle lightly with dressing. Garnish with cilantro.

MAKES 4 GENEROUS SERVINGS

Chinese Barbecued Pork Salad with Crisp Vegetables and Hoisin Vinaigrette

No need to take a course in Asian cooking for this casually assembled salad: already-cooked, excellent-quality *char siu*—Chinese barbecued pork—is readily available in Chinese markets or as take-out from good-sized Cantonese-style restaurants. You can purchase the other ingredients at your Asian market, too, though they're available fairly readily in most well-stocked supermarkets.

HOISIN VINAIGRETTE
¼ cup hoisin sauce
1 tablespoon lemon juice
1 tablespoon rice vinegar
½ cup peanut oil
1 teaspoon sesame oil

SALAD
1½ pounds *char siu* (Chinese barbecued pork), cut into ¼-inch-thick slices
4 cups coarsely shredded napa cabbage leaves
4 cups coarsely shredded bok choy
4 medium-sized scallions, sliced thin lengthwise and cut crosswise into 1-inch pieces
2 large carrots, shredded coarse
1 medium-sized red bell pepper, halved, stemmed, seeded, and cut into ¼-by-1-inch matchsticks
1 medium-sized green bell pepper, halved, stemmed, seeded, and cut into ¼-by-1-inch matchsticks
16 large oak leaf lettuce leaves
¼ cup coarsely chopped cilantro
2 tablespoons white sesame seeds, toasted (see Index), or black sesame seeds

1. *Make dressing:* In a mixing bowl, stir together hoisin, lemon juice, and vinegar. Whisking continuously, slowly stir in peanut and sesame oils. Set aside.

2. *Toss and arrange salad:* In a mixing bowl, toss together pork, cabbage, bok choy, scallions, carrots, and peppers with enough dressing to coat. Arrange lettuce leaves on a platter or individual serving plates. Mound salad in center and garnish with cilantro and sesame seeds.

MAKES 4 GENEROUS SERVINGS

Cajun Andouille Sausage Salad with Baby Greens and Spicy Pecan Vinaigrette

You'll find spicy Cajun-style andouille sausage in most good butcher shops and gourmet markets; hot Italian pork sausage is an acceptable substitute.

SPICY PECAN VINAIGRETTE

2 tablespoons balsamic vinegar
2 tablespoons lemon juice
2 tablespoons creamy Dijon-style mustard
2 tablespoons finely chopped pecans
½ teaspoon Tabasco sauce
¼ teaspoon sugar
¼ teaspoon salt
¼ teaspoon white pepper
½ cup olive oil
¼ cup walnut oil

SALAD

4 fresh andouille sausages
12 cups mixed baby salad leaves (see Index)
1 large red bell pepper, halved, stemmed, seeded, and cut crosswise into ¼-inch-wide strips
1 large yellow bell pepper, halved, stemmed, seeded, and cut crosswise into ¼-inch-wide strips
1 large Vidalia, Maui, Walla Walla, or sweet red onion, cut into ¼-inch-thick slices
4 large ripe Roma tomatoes, cored and quartered
½ cup pecan halves, toasted (see Index)
2 tablespoons finely chopped fresh chives
2 tablespoons finely chopped Italian parsley

1. *Make dressing:* In a bowl, stir together vinegar, lemon juice, mustard, pecans, Tabasco, sugar, salt, and pepper. Whisking continuously, slowly pour in olive and walnut oils until blended. Set aside.

2. *Cook sausages:* Put sausages in a saucepan of cold water. Bring to a boil over moderate heat. Meanwhile, preheat grill or broiler until very hot. Drain sausages and grill until seared golden brown, 3 to 4 minutes per side.

3. *Arrange salad:* In a mixing bowl, toss salad leaves, peppers, and onion with just enough dressing to coat. Arrange in beds on individual serving plates. Cut each sausage diagonally into ½-inch-thick slices and array across each salad. Place tomato wedges around sausage slices; scatter pecans over and around sausage. Drizzle with more dressing and garnish with chives and parsley.

MAKES 4 GENEROUS SERVINGS

4

CHEESE AND EGG SALADS

Dairy Chef's Salad with Cider Honey Vinaigrette

Nouvelle Tricolore Salad with Buffalo Mozzarella, Tomatoes, Avocado,
Three Greens, and Basil Pesto Vinaigrette

Grilled Quesadilla Salad with Grilled Scallions and Cilantro Vinaigrette

Insalata Parmigiana with Italian Country Greens, Roasted Peppers,
Garlic Croutons, and Grainy Dijon Mustard Vinaigrette

Baked Almond-Crusted Camembert Salad with Watercress,
Apples, Pears, and Creamy Dijon Mustard Vinaigrette

Broiled Goat Cheese Salad with Sun-Dried Tomatoes, Belgian Endive,
Oak Leaf Lettuce, and Hazelnut Vinaigrette

Poached Eggs in Crisp Vegetable Nests with Grainy Dijon Mustard Vinaigrette

Salad of Fresh Creamy Goat Cheese, Bitter Lettuces,
Sun-Dried Tomatoes, and Garlic Herb Croutons

Poached Eggs on a Bed of Bitter Greens with Balsamic Vinaigrette

Anchovy-Filled Deviled Egg Salad on a Bed of Baby Greens
with a Light Lemon Herb Vinaigrette

Classic Egg Salad with Neoclassical Companions

Dairy Chef's Salad with Cider Honey Vinaigrette

For those who shun meat but don't want to forgo traditional salad pleasures, this all-dairy version of a chef's salad satisfies well. The sweet-spicy dressing both highlights and slightly tones down the richness of the cheeses.

CIDER HONEY VINAIGRETTE
See Index

SALAD

6 cups coarsely chopped romaine lettuce leaves
6 cups coarsely chopped iceberg lettuce leaves
¼ pound thinly sliced sharp cheddar cheese, cut into ½-inch-wide strips
¼ pound thinly sliced provolone cheese, cut into ½-inch-wide strips
¼ pound thinly sliced smoked Gouda cheese, cut into ½-inch-wide strips
¼ pound blue cheese, crumbled
½ cup blanched slivered almonds, toasted (see Index)
4 hard-boiled eggs, quartered lengthwise
16 cherry tomatoes, stemmed and halved

1. *Make dressing:* See Index for Cider Honey Vinaigrette.
2. *Arrange and serve salad:* Toss together romaine and iceberg and arrange in beds in large individual salad bowls. Arrange cheese strips and crumbled blue cheese decoratively on top of lettuces. Scatter almonds over cheese and place eggs and tomatoes on top. Pass dressing on the side.

MAKES 4 GENEROUS SERVINGS

Nouvelle Tricolore Salad with Buffalo Mozzarella, Tomatoes, Avocado, Three Greens, and Basil Pesto Vinaigrette

The traditional Italian tricolore salad displays the three colors of the Italian flag with its red tomatoes, white mozzarella cheese, and green basil leaves. This updated and expanded version doubles up on every color—adding the red of sun-dried tomatoes, the white of fresh mushrooms, and the green of avocado. In addition, it presents the composition on a tricolored bed of greens.

BASIL PESTO VINAIGRETTE
See Index

SALAD

12 baby radicchio leaves
12 baby Belgian endive leaves
12 baby oak leaf lettuce leaves
1 pound fresh buffalo mozzarella, cut into 16 neat wedges
4 large firm ripe Roma tomatoes, cored and quartered
1 large firm ripe Haas avocado

½ cup packed drained sun-dried tomatoes, cut into ¼-inch-wide slivers
12 medium-sized field mushrooms, cut into ¼-inch-thick slices
4 tablespoons finely shredded fresh basil leaves

1. *Make dressing:* See Index for Basil Pesto Vinaigrette.
2. *Arrange salad:* On individual serving plates, arrange radicchio, endive, and lettuce leaves in attractive patterns. Place mozzarella and tomatoes evenly on top. Halve, pit, and peel avocado; cut lengthwise into thin slices and arrange slices on each salad. Scatter sun-dried tomatoes and mushroom slices on top. Drizzle with dressing and garnish with fresh basil.

MAKES 4 GENEROUS SERVINGS

Grilled Quesadilla Salad with Grilled Scallions and Cilantro Vinaigrette

The simple and very popular Mexican *antojito,* or appetizer, of a folded flour tortilla filled with cheese and grilled becomes the centerpiece of this appealing main-course salad. Feel free to vary the cheeses according to your taste and whim.

CILANTRO VINAIGRETTE
2 tablespoons balsamic vinegar
2 tablespoons lemon juice
2 tablespoons finely chopped cilantro
1 teaspoon coarse-grained Dijon-style
  mustard
¼ teaspoon sugar
¼ teaspoon salt
¼ teaspoon white pepper
¾ cup olive oil

GRILLED QUESADILLAS AND GRILLED SCALLIONS
4 large flour tortillas
¼ pound sharp cheddar cheese, shredded
  coarse
¼ pound plain or pepper-flavored
  Monterey Jack cheese, shredded coarse
2 tablespoons finely chopped cilantro
¼ cup olive oil
8 medium-sized whole scallions, ends
  trimmed
Salt
Black pepper

SALAD
4 cups coarsely torn radicchio leaves
4 cups coarsely torn Bibb lettuce leaves
4 cups coarsely torn romaine lettuce
  leaves
½ cup pine nuts, toasted (see Index)
6 firm ripe Roma tomatoes, cored and
  cut into ½- to ¾-inch chunks
2 tablespoons finely chopped fresh
  chives
2 tablespoons finely chopped fresh
  Italian parsley

1. *Make dressing:* In a mixing bowl, stir together vinegar, lemon juice, cilantro, mustard, sugar, salt, and pepper. Whisking continuously, slowly pour in oil until blended. Set aside.

2. *Grill quesadillas and scallions:* Preheat grill or broiler until very hot. Place tortillas on a work surface and sprinkle cheeses evenly over one half of each; scatter cilantro over cheese and fold tortillas over to enclose cheese. Lightly brush tortillas and scallions with oil; season scallions with salt and pepper. Grill or broil until tortillas are crisp, golden brown, and cheese is melted and until scallions are golden brown, 2 to 3 minutes per side.

3. *Toss and arrange salad:* In a mixing bowl, toss radicchio, Bibb, romaine, pine nuts, and tomatoes with enough dressing to coat; arrange in beds on individual serving plates. Cut each quesadilla into 4 wedges and transfer to center of salads; place scallions alongside. Garnish with chives and parsley.

MAKES 4 GENEROUS SERVINGS

Insalata Parmigiana with Italian Country Greens, Roasted Peppers, Garlic Croutons, and Grainy Dijon Mustard Vinaigrette

I could happily sit down and eat my way through a block of good-quality imported Italian Parmesan—so satisfying and complex in its flavor. That's why I think this salad, which contrasts generous shavings of the cheese with bitter rocket (also known by the Italian name arugula) and radicchio leaves, works so well as a luncheon main course.

GRAINY DIJON MUSTARD
VINAIGRETTE
See Index

SALAD
6 cups coarsely torn radicchio leaves
6 cups coarsely torn rocket leaves
1 large red bell pepper, roasted, stemmed, peeled, seeded (see Index), and torn into long thin strips
1½ cups garlic croutons (see Index)

½ pound block imported Italian Parmesan cheese, cut into thin shavings with a vegetable peeler or small sharp knife
Coarsely ground black pepper

1. *Make dressing:* See Index for Grainy Dijon Mustard Vinaigrette.

2. *Toss and arrange salad:* In a mixing bowl, toss radicchio, rocket, pepper strips, and croutons with enough dressing to coat. Arrange on individual serving plates and scatter Parmesan shavings on top. Sprinkle with black pepper.

MAKES 4 GENEROUS SERVINGS

Baked Almond-Crusted Camembert Salad with Watercress, Apples, Pears, and Creamy Dijon Mustard Vinaigrette

Rich and satisfying, yet light, this salad makes a delightful luncheon main course.

CREAMY DIJON MUSTARD
VINAIGRETTE
See Index

BAKED ALMOND-CRUSTED
CAMEMBERT
1 whole 8- to 12-ounce Camembert
cheese, ripe but firm
½ cup slivered blanched almonds

SALAD
12 cups watercress sprigs
2 large firm ripe apples, cored, sliced thin,
and tossed with 2 tablespoons lemon
juice
2 large firm ripe pears, cored, sliced thin,
and tossed with 2 tablespoons lemon
juice
2 tablespoons finely chopped fresh chives
2 tablespoons finely chopped Italian parsley

1. *Make dressing:* See Index for Creamy Dijon Mustard Vinaigrette.

2. *Bake Camembert:* Preheat the oven to 375°F. With a long, sharp bread knife, carefully cut off the top rind of the cheese. Place cheese, cut side up, in a lightly greased baking dish. Press almonds evenly into top of cheese. Bake until almonds are golden brown and cheese is heated through, 12 to 15 minutes.

3. *Toss and arrange salad:* Toss watercress with enough dressing to coat. Arrange in beds on individual serving plates. Cut Camembert into 4 equal wedges and, with a spatula, quickly transfer to plates on top of watercress. Arrange apple and pear slices around cheese. Garnish cheese and fruit with chives and parsley.

MAKES 4 GENEROUS SERVINGS

Broiled Goat Cheese Salad with Sun-Dried Tomatoes, Belgian Endive, Oak Leaf Lettuce, and Hazelnut Vinaigrette

A virtual classic of contemporary cooking, this salad calls for one of the fairly common cylinder-shaped aged goat cheeses produced both in France and in the United States.

HAZELNUT VINAIGRETTE
2 tablespoons sherry vinegar
2 tablespoons coarse-grained Dijon-style mustard
½ teaspoon sugar
½ teaspoon salt
½ teaspoon white pepper
¼ cup hazelnut oil
¼ cup olive oil

BROILED GOAT CHEESE
¼ cup hazelnut oil
¾ pound aged cylindrical goat cheese, cut into 8 equal rounds
Salt
Black pepper

SALAD
20 small to medium-sized oak leaf lettuce leaves
5 cups thinly sliced Belgian endive leaves
½ cup drained sun-dried tomatoes, cut into ¼-inch-wide strips
½ cup coarsely broken hazelnuts, toasted (see Index)
¾ cup garlic croutons (see Index)
2 tablespoons finely chopped fresh chives
1 tablespoon finely chopped fresh parsley

1. *Make vinaigrette:* In a mixing bowl, stir together vinegar, mustard, sugar, salt, and pepper. Whisking continuously, very slowly pour in oils until blended. Set aside.

2. *Broil goat cheese:* Preheat broiler until very hot. Pour hazelnut oil into a shallow baking dish to coat bottom. Place cheese rounds in dish and sprinkle with salt and pepper. Broil until golden brown, 3 to 4 minutes.

3. *Arrange salad:* While cheese is broiling, arrange lettuce leaves in beds on individual serving plates. Toss endive with just enough dressing to coat and arrange in center of each plate. When cheese is ready, use a spatula to carefully transfer 2 rounds to each plate. Drizzle a little dressing over cheese and scatter sun-dried tomatoes and hazelnuts over cheese and endive. Scatter croutons around cheese. Garnish with chives and parsley.

MAKES 4 GENEROUS SERVINGS

Poached Eggs in Crisp Vegetable Nests with Grainy Dijon Mustard Vinaigrette

Eye-catchingly beautiful, this simple, fresh-tasting luncheon salad presents poached eggs in nests fashioned from long, thin julienne strips of vegetables.

GRAINY DIJON MUSTARD
VINAIGRETTE
See Index

SALAD

1 medium-sized cucumber, peeled, halved lengthwise, seeded, and cut lengthwise into long thin julienne strips

1 medium-sized carrot, peeled and cut lengthwise into long thin julienne strips

½ pound jicama, peeled and cut into long thin julienne strips

1 small red bell pepper, halved, stemmed, seeded, and cut into long thin julienne strips

1 small green bell pepper, halved, stemmed, seeded, and cut into long thin julienne strips

12 Bibb lettuce leaves

½ cup white vinegar

8 large eggs

1 tablespoon finely chopped fresh chives

1 tablespoon finely chopped fresh Italian parsley

1. *Make vinaigrette:* See Index for Grainy Dijon Mustard Vinaigrette.

2. *Assemble nests:* In a mixing bowl, toss cucumber, carrot, jicama, and bell peppers with just enough dressing to coat. Place lettuce leaves on individual serving plates and, in center of each, arrange shredded vegetables to form a circular nest with a large indentation in the middle.

3. *Poach eggs and serve salad:* In a shallow saucepan, bring 1 to 2 inches water to a boil; add vinegar and reduce heat to maintain a bare simmer. One at a time, break eggs carefully into water, without overcrowding. Poach each egg for 3 minutes, until white is firm but yolk is still liquid; carefully lift out with a slotted spoon and drain on paper towels. With a knife, trim any ragged edges of egg white. Carefully transfer 2 eggs to center of each nest. Drizzle eggs with a little dressing and garnish with chives and parsley.

MAKES 4 GENEROUS SERVINGS

Salad of Fresh Creamy Goat Cheese, Bitter Lettuces, Sun-Dried Tomatoes, and Garlic Herb Croutons

Thankfully, a wide variety of goat cheeses have become fairly commonplace items in gourmet stores and upscale supermarkets in recent years. Try one of the wonderful fresh goat cheeses now coming out of northern California—so rich and creamy that they're capable of starring in this simple main-course salad.

BALSAMIC VINAIGRETTE
See Index

SALAD
4 cups coarsely torn curly endive leaves
4 cups coarsely torn radicchio leaves
4 cups coarsely torn rocket leaves
¾ cup packed drained sun-dried
  tomatoes, cut into ¼-inch-wide slivers
¾ cup garlic herb croutons (see Index)
¾ pound fresh creamy goat cheese
2 tablespoons finely chopped fresh
  chives

1. *Make dressing:* See Index for Balsamic Vinaigrette.
2. *Toss and arrange salad:* In a mixing bowl, toss endive, radicchio, rocket, sun-dried tomatoes, and croutons with enough dressing to coat. Scatter goat cheese in small clumps over salad. Garnish with chives.

MAKES 4 GENEROUS SERVINGS

Poached Eggs on a Bed of Bitter Greens
with Balsamic Vinaigrette

The creaminess of the still-liquid poached yolks contrasts wonderfully with the bed of crisp, slightly bitter-tasting greens that forms the base of this salad.

BALSAMIC VINAIGRETTE
See Index

SALAD
½ cup white vinegar
8 large eggs
4 cups thinly sliced Belgian endive leaves
4 cups watercress, separated into small
   sprigs
4 cups rocket leaves
1 tablespoon finely chopped fresh chives
1 tablespoon finely chopped fresh Italian
   parsley

1. *Make vinaigrette:* See Index for Balsamic Vinaigrette.

2. *Poach eggs:* In a shallow saucepan, bring 1 to 2 inches water to a boil; add vinegar and reduce heat to maintain a bare simmer. One at a time, break eggs carefully into water, without overcrowding. Poach each egg for 3 minutes, until white is firm but yolk is still liquid; carefully lift out with a slotted spoon and drain on paper towels. With a knife, trim any ragged edges of egg white.

3. *Assemble salad:* In a mixing bowl, toss endive, watercress, and rocket together with enough dressing to coat; arrange in beds on individual serving plates. Carefully transfer 2 eggs to center of each plate. Drizzle eggs with a little dressing and garnish with chives and parsley.

MAKES 4 GENEROUS SERVINGS

Anchovy-Filled Deviled Egg Salad on a Bed of Baby Greens with a Light Lemon Herb Vinaigrette

Serve this salad as a light luncheon main course on a sunny day. If you don't like anchovies, you can certainly leave them out of the egg-yolk mixture.

LIGHT LEMON HERB
VINAIGRETTE
See Index

SALAD

12 hard-boiled eggs, halved lengthwise
6 tablespoons mayonnaise
2 tablespoons coarse-grained Dijon-style mustard
1 tablespoon lemon juice
6 anchovy fillets, chopped coarse
2 tablespoons finely chopped fresh chives
1 tablespoon finely chopped fresh chervil

24 capers, drained
10 cups mixed baby salad leaves
1 red bell pepper, roasted, stemmed, peeled, seeded (see Index), and torn into thin strips
1 yellow bell pepper, roasted, stemmed, peeled, seeded (see Index), and torn into thin strips
Fresh Italian parsley sprigs

1. *Make dressing:* See Index for Light Lemon Herb Vinaigrette.

2. *Stuff eggs:* In a mixing bowl, mash together hard-boiled egg yolks, mayonnaise, mustard, lemon juice, anchovies, and herbs. Spoon mixture into a piping bag fitted with a star tip and pipe back into egg halves; or neatly spoon mixture back in. Dot yolk of each egg half with a caper.

3. *Arrange salad:* Toss salad leaves with enough dressing to coat and arrange decoratively on a large platter or individual serving plates. Arrange eggs on top of leaves and strew pepper strips decoratively among them. Garnish with parsley sprigs.

MAKES 4 GENEROUS SERVINGS

Classic Egg Salad with Neoclassical Companions

Although it is unimpeachably perfect in its way, I've always found the classic mayonnaise-bound egg salad a little bit overwhelming—particularly when it is served as a main-course dish, an unremittingly creamy scoop of it surrounded by a sea of lettuce. But I find that some of the signature ingredients of contemporary cuisine go a long way toward providing contrast and relief, while filling out the egg salad to a truly satisfying main course.

CLASSIC EGG SALAD
12 hard-boiled eggs, yolks and whites
  separated and chopped fine
2 tablespoons creamy Dijon-style
  mustard
1 tablespoon lemon juice
1 tablespoon finely chopped fresh chives
1 tablespoon finely chopped fresh dill
1 tablespoon finely chopped fresh
  parsley
¼ teaspoon salt
¼ teaspoon white pepper
¾ cup mayonnaise

SALAD
12 baby radicchio leaves
12 baby lamb's lettuce leaves
12 baby Bibb lettuce leaves
12 baby oak leaf lettuce leaves
1 firm ripe Haas avocado
2 firm ripe kiwifruits, peeled and sliced
  thin
1 large ripe papaya, halved, seeded,
  peeled, and sliced thin lengthwise
2 tablespoons golden caviar

1. *Make egg salad:* In a mixing bowl, thoroughly combine eggs, mustard, lemon juice, herbs, salt, and pepper with enough mayonnaise to bind the mixture well. Cover and refrigerate.

2. *Arrange salad:* Before serving, arrange baby radicchio and lettuces in attractive patterns on individual serving plates. Mound egg salad in center of each plate. Halve, pit, and peel avocado and slice thin lengthwise. Arrange avocado, kiwi, and papaya slices around egg salad. Top each mound of egg salad with golden caviar.

MAKES 4 GENEROUS SERVINGS

5

PASTA AND GRAIN SALADS

Pasta Salad Primavera with Fines Herbes Vinaigrette

Smoked Salmon Spaghetti Salad with Lemon Caper Vinaigrette

Bay Shrimp Salad with Shells and Light Lemon Herb Vinaigrette

Crab and Slivered Vegetable Pasta Salad with
Mustard–Fines Herbes Mayonnaise

Chicken Couscous Salad with Dried Fruits, Almonds,
and Lemon-Mint-Honey Dressing

Wagon Wheel Pasta Salad with Smoked Chicken, Apples, Peppers,
and Sun-Dried Tomato Pesto Vinaigrette

Bow Tie Pasta Salad with Grilled Chicken,
Springtime Vegetables, and Creamy Dijon Mustard Vinaigrette

Curried Chicken Pasta Salad with Sherried Chutney Mayonnaise

Turkey and Wild Rice Salad
with Sweet-Hot Walnut Oil Vinaigrette on a Bed of Cabbage

Orzo Salad with Turkey Sausage,
Raisins, Pine Nuts, and Lemon-Mint-Honey Dressing

Szechuan Noodle Salad with Shredded Meat and Vegetables
and Spicy Sesame Peanut Dressing

Veal Tortellini Salad with Peppers, Pine Nuts, and Basil Pesto Vinaigrette

Lamb Tabbouleh Salad

Macaroni Salad with Ham, Roasted Peppers, Gruyère,
and Dijon Mustard Mayonnaise

Chinese Rice Noodle Salad with Slivered Pork, Crisp Asparagus,
and Lemon–Sesame Seed Dressing

Deli Pasta Salad with Honey-Mustard-Dill Vinaigrette

Antipasto Pasta with Herbed Parmesan Vinaigrette

Pasta Salad Primavera with Fines Herbes Vinaigrette

Springtime-fresh vegetables are highlighted in this luncheon salad. Allow time for the vegetables to marinate in the vinaigrette dressing before tossing with the pasta.

FINES HERBES VINAIGRETTE

¾ cup plus 2 tablespoons olive oil
¼ cup white-wine vinegar
2 tablespoons lemon juice
½ tablespoon prepared creamy Dijon-style mustard
1 teaspoon finely chopped fresh chervil
1 teaspoon finely chopped fresh chives
1 teaspoon finely chopped fresh dill
1 teaspoon finely chopped fresh Italian parsley
½ teaspoon salt
½ teaspoon white pepper

SALAD

1 cup broccoli florets, boiled until tender-crisp, drained very well
1 cup carrots cut diagonally into ¼-inch slices, boiled until tender-crisp, drained very well
1 cup small snow peas, boiled until tender-crisp, drained very well
1 medium-sized zucchini, cut crosswise into ¼-inch slices
1 medium-sized yellow summer squash, cut crosswise into ¼-inch slices
10 cups cooked multicolored or plain rotini (spiral-shaped) pasta (about 1¼ pounds dry), al dente, drained, rinsed, and cooled
¼ pound block Parmesan cheese, cut into thin 1-inch-long shavings with a vegetable peeler or small, sharp knife
1 large red bell pepper, stemmed, seeded, and cut into ¼- to ½-inch dice
2 medium-sized scallions, sliced thin crosswise
24 radicchio or small romaine lettuce leaves
8 fresh basil leaves, cut crosswise into thin julienne strips

1. *Make dressing:* Combine all ingredients in a jar with a tight-fitting lid. Shake well. Pour into a large mixing bowl.

2. *Marinate vegetables:* Put broccoli, carrots, snow peas, zucchini, and yellow squash in large mixing bowl with dressing. Toss well to coat. Cover and refrigerate 1 to 2 hours, turning vegetables several times.

3. *Toss and serve salad:* Add pasta, Parmesan, bell pepper, and scallions to mixing bowl. Toss well. Arrange radicchio or romaine leaves on a platter or large serving plates and mound salad on top. Garnish with basil.

MAKES 4 GENEROUS SERVINGS

Smoked Salmon Spaghetti Salad with Lemon Caper Vinaigrette

Not surprisingly, this makes a great brunchtime salad.

LEMON CAPER VINAIGRETTE
1 medium-sized shallot, peeled
1 medium-sized garlic clove, peeled
¾ cup olive oil
¼ cup lemon juice
¼ cup drained capers
1 tablespoon dried oregano
½ teaspoon white pepper

SALAD
10 cups cooked spaghetti (about 1¼ pounds
  dry), al dente, drained, rinsed, and cooled
¾ pound thinly sliced smoked salmon, cut
  into long thin strips
1 large cucumber, peeled, halved
  lengthwise, seeded, and cut into long
  thin shreds
1 medium-sized red onion, sliced very thin
6 tablespoons finely chopped Italian parsley
16 Bibb lettuce leaves
4 firm ripe Roma tomatoes, cut into 4
  wedges each
Fresh parsley sprigs

1. *Make dressing:* Put shallot and garlic in a food processor with the metal blade. Pulse until finely chopped, stopping 2 or 3 times to scrape down bowl. Add remaining ingredients and pulse just until blended and capers are very coarsely chopped. Set aside.

2. *Toss and arrange salad:* In a mixing bowl, toss spaghetti, salmon, cucumber, onion, and chopped parsley with enough dressing to coat. Arrange lettuce leaves on a platter or individual serving plates. Mound salad in center and place tomato wedges around sides. Garnish with parsley sprigs.

MAKES 4 GENEROUS SERVINGS

Bay Shrimp Salad with Shells and Light Lemon Herb Vinaigrette

The light, herb-flecked vinaigrette and tender-crisp vegetables contrast nicely with the sweet, tender bay shrimp and al dente pasta in this refreshing luncheon salad.

LIGHT LEMON HERB
VINAIGRETTE
See Index

SALAD

10 cups cooked small to medium-sized pasta shells (about 1¼ pounds dry), al dente, drained, rinsed, and cooled

1½ cups small snow peas, boiled until tender-crisp, drained, rinsed, and cooled

¼ cup finely chopped fresh chives

1½ pounds cooked baby bay shrimp

2 large celery stalks, cut crosswise into thin strips

1 medium-sized red bell pepper, halved, stemmed, seeded, and cut into ¼-inch dice

1 medium-sized green bell pepper, halved, stemmed, seeded, and cut into ¼-inch dice

6 cups shredded romaine lettuce leaves, chilled in the refrigerator

Fresh parsley sprigs

1. *Make dressing:* See Index for Light Lemon Herb Vinaigrette.

2. *Toss and arrange salad:* In a mixing bowl, toss together pasta, snow peas, chives, shrimp, celery, and bell peppers with enough dressing to coat well. Arrange romaine on a platter or individual serving plates and mound salad on top. Garnish with parsley.

MAKES 4 GENEROUS SERVINGS

Crab and Slivered Vegetable Pasta Salad with Mustard–Fines Herbes Mayonnaise

The texture of flaked crabmeat, I find, goes particularly well with cooked pasta in a salad. This one includes a dressing flavored with Dijon mustard and fresh herbs, which highlight the crab's flavor.

MUSTARD–FINES HERBES MAYONNAISE

1⅓ cups mayonnaise

2 tablespoons creamy Dijon-style mustard

2 tablespoons finely chopped fresh dill

2 tablespoons finely chopped fresh Italian parsley

2 tablespoons finely chopped fresh chives

1 tablespoon finely chopped fresh tarragon

1 tablespoon lemon juice

SALAD

10 cups cooked medium-sized pasta shells (about 1¼ pounds dry), al dente, drained, rinsed, and cooled

1½ pounds cooked crabmeat, flaked and picked clean of shell and cartilage

1½ cups snow peas, trimmed, parboiled until tender-crisp, and cut diagonally into ¼-inch-wide slivers

2 red bell peppers, quartered, stemmed, seeded, and cut crosswise into ¼-inch-wide strips

2 carrots, cut lengthwise into thin slices, then diagonally into ¼-inch-wide slivers

6 cups small butter lettuce leaves, chilled in refrigerator

12 cooked cocktail-style crab claws (optional)

12 parsley sprigs

1. *Make dressing:* In a mixing bowl, stir together mayonnaise, mustard, herbs, and lemon juice. Set aside.

2. *Prepare and assemble salad:* In a large mixing bowl, combine all salad ingredients except butter lettuce, crab claws, and parsley sprigs. Toss well, adding enough dressing to coat ingredients. Arrange lettuce on a large platter or individual serving plates and mound salad on top. Garnish with crab claws and parsley.

MAKES 4 GENEROUS SERVINGS

Chicken Couscous Salad with Dried Fruits, Almonds, and Lemon-Mint-Honey Dressing

Inspired by the well-known Moroccan specialty based on steamed fine-grained semolina, this light yet filling salad features chunks of grilled chicken accompanied by dried fruits and an aromatic dressing that reflect a North African influence. Couscous is available in Middle Eastern markets and in the gourmet food section of well-stocked supermarkets.

LEMON-MINT-HONEY DRESSING
6 tablespoons lemon juice
2 tablespoons honey, at room
   temperature
2 tablespoons finely chopped fresh mint
½ teaspoon salt
¼ teaspoon white pepper
1¼ cups olive oil

SALAD
8 cups (about 3 cups dry) steamed
   couscous, fluffed with a fork and
   cooled
2 cups coarsely chopped cooked chicken
¾ cup dried apricots, soaked in hot
   water to cover for 10 minutes, drained,
   and cut into ¼-inch-wide slices
¾ cup pitted dates, chopped coarse
¾ cup slivered blanched almonds,
   toasted (see Index)
24 Belgian endive leaves
Fresh mint sprigs

1. *Make dressing:* In a mixing bowl, stir together lemon, honey, mint, salt, and pepper. Whisking continuously, slowly pour in oil until blended. Set aside.

2. *Toss and arrange salad:* In a mixing bowl, lightly toss together couscous, chicken, apricots, dates, and almonds with enough dressing to coat well. Arrange endive leaves like spokes around the edge of a platter or individual serving plates. Mound salad in center. Garnish with mint.

MAKES 4 GENEROUS SERVINGS

Wagon Wheel Pasta Salad
with Smoked Chicken, Apples, Peppers, and Sun-Dried Tomato Pesto Vinaigrette

This lively combination of ingredients features the widely available pasta shaped like little wagon wheels. If you can't find it, substitute pasta bow ties, medium-sized shells, or spirals.

SUN-DRIED TOMATO PESTO
VINAIGRETTE
See Index

SALAD

10 cups cooked wagon wheel pasta (about 1¼ pounds dry), al dente, drained, rinsed, and cooled

1 pound smoked chicken, cut into ¼-inch-thick slivers

2 medium-sized tart green eating apples, cored and cut into ½-inch pieces

2 medium-sized celery stalks, cut crosswise into ¼-inch-thick slices

1 large red bell pepper, halved, stemmed, seeded, and cut into ½-inch dice

24 radicchio leaves

¼ cup pine nuts, toasted (see Index)

¼ cup coarsely chopped Italian parsley

1. *Make dressing:* See Index for Sun-Dried Tomato Pesto Vinaigrette.

2. *Prepare and assemble salad:* In a mixing bowl, combine all salad ingredients except radicchio, pine nuts, and parsley. Toss well with enough dressing to coat. Arrange radicchio leaves on a platter or individual serving plates. Mound salad on top. Garnish with pine nuts and parsley.

MAKES 4 GENEROUS SERVINGS

Bow Tie Pasta Salad with Grilled Chicken, Springtime Vegetables, and Creamy Dijon Mustard Vinaigrette

Serve this salad at a casual luncheon that calls for something a little more special.

CREAMY DIJON MUSTARD
VINAIGRETTE
See Index

GRILLED CHICKEN
3 tablespoons lemon juice
2 tablespoons olive oil
1 teaspoon dried rosemary
4 large boneless skinless chicken breast
   halves
Salt
Black pepper

SALAD
10 cups cooked bow tie pasta (about 1¼
   pounds dry), al dente, drained, rinsed,
   and cooled
1½ cups shelled peas, boiled just until
   tender, drained, and cooled
¼ cup finely chopped fresh chives
¼ cup finely chopped fresh chervil or
   Italian parsley
2 medium-sized carrots, diagonally
   sliced thin, boiled until tender-crisp,
   drained, and cooled
2 medium-sized red bell peppers,
   roasted, peeled, seeded (see Index),
   and torn into thin strips
24 radicchio leaves
¼ pound block Parmesan cheese, cut
   into thin shavings with a vegetable
   peeler or a small sharp knife
Fresh chervil or parsley sprigs

1. *Make dressing:* See Index for Creamy Dijon Mustard Vinaigrette.

2. *Marinate chicken:* In a shallow bowl, stir together lemon juice, olive oil, and rosemary. Turn chicken in bowl to coat; marinate 15 to 30 minutes.

3. *Grill chicken:* Preheat grill or broiler until very hot. Season chicken with salt and pepper and grill until cooked through and golden brown, 4 to 5 minutes per side, basting with marinade before turning.

4. *Toss and arrange salad:* In a mixing bowl, toss together pasta, peas, chopped chives and chervil, carrots, and peppers with enough dressing to coat. Arrange radicchio leaves on individual serving plates and spread salad in center. Cut each chicken breast crosswise into ½-inch-wide pieces and place on top of pasta. Spoon a little dressing over chicken and garnish with Parmesan shavings and chervil or parsley sprigs.

MAKES 4 GENEROUS SERVINGS

Curried Chicken Pasta Salad
with Sherried Chutney Mayonnaise

For those who like a bit of spicy sweetness to their pasta salads, this subtle blend is just right. It's a great salad to make with those preroasted chickens so many supermarkets sell today.

SHERRIED CHUTNEY
MAYONNAISE
1 cup mayonnaise
½ cup bottled mango chutney or mixed-fruit chutney, fruit pieces chopped fine
3 tablespoons dry sherry

SALAD
10 cups cooked small or medium-sized pasta shells (about 1¼ pounds dry), al dente, drained, rinsed, and cooled
1½ pounds cooked chicken meat, cut or torn into 1-inch chunks
1½ cups seedless red or green grapes, cut into halves
¾ cup slivered blanched almonds, toasted (see Index)
½ cup seedless golden or dark raisins
½ cup shredded coconut, toasted (see Index)
2 scallions, sliced thin crosswise
2 celery stalks, cut crosswise into ¼-inch slices
6 cups thinly shredded romaine lettuce leaves, chilled in refrigerator
¼ cup coarsely chopped cilantro

1. *Make dressing:* In a mixing bowl, stir together mayonnaise, chutney, and sherry. Set aside.

2. *Prepare and assemble salad:* In a mixing bowl, combine all salad ingredients except romaine lettuce and cilantro. Toss well with enough dressing to coat. Spread romaine on a large platter or individual serving plates and arrange salad on top. Garnish with cilantro.

MAKES 4 GENEROUS SERVINGS

Turkey and Wild Rice Salad with Sweet-Hot Walnut Oil Vinaigrette on a Bed of Cabbage

Transform those inevitable turkey leftovers into this wonderfully delicious salad.

SWEET-HOT WALNUT OIL
VINAIGRETTE
¾ cup walnut oil
½ cup olive oil
⅓ cup cider vinegar
3 tablespoons honey
3 tablespoons prepared English-style
   mustard
¼ teaspoon salt
¼ teaspoon white pepper

SALAD
4 cups cooked wild rice (about 1½ cups
   uncooked)
4 cups cooked basmati or long-grain white
   rice (about 1⅓ cups uncooked)
3 cups coarsely chopped cooked turkey
   meat
1 cup coarsely chopped dried apricots
¾ cup coarsely chopped pecans, toasted
   (see Index)
½ cup finely chopped Italian parsley
4 scallions, sliced thin crosswise
1 large red bell pepper, halved, stemmed,
   seeded, and cut into ¼-inch dice
3 cups finely shredded red cabbage leaves
3 cups finely shredded savoy cabbage
   leaves
Fresh parsley sprigs

   1. *Make dressing:* Combine all ingredients in a jar with a tight-fitting lid. Shake well. Set aside.
   2. *Toss and arrange salad:* In a large mixing bowl toss all ingredients except cabbages with enough dressing to coat well. Toss together cabbage shreds with a little remaining dressing and arrange in a bed on a platter or large individual plates. Mound salad mixture on top. Garnish with parsley sprigs.

MAKES 4 GENEROUS SERVINGS

130

Orzo Salad with Turkey Sausage, Raisins, Pine Nuts, and Lemon-Mint-Honey Dressing

The small rice-shaped pasta known as orzo becomes the foundation for a sweet-spicy salad featuring the excellent-quality fresh turkey sausage that has come into vogue in recent years. You can, if you like or if necessary, substitute pork or chicken sausage.

LEMON-MINT-HONEY DRESSING
See Index

SALAD

1½ pounds fresh sweet or spicy Italian-style turkey sausage, casings peeled off
10 cups cooked orzo (about 1¼ pounds dry), al dente, drained, rinsed, and cooled
¾ cup pine nuts, toasted (see Index)
½ cup seedless brown or golden raisins
½ cup finely chopped Italian parsley
½ cup finely chopped fresh chives
1 large red bell pepper, halved, stemmed, seeded, and cut into ½-inch squares
24 Bibb lettuce leaves
6 firm ripe Roma tomatoes, cored and cut into 4 wedges each
Fresh mint or parsley sprigs

1. *Make dressing:* See Index for Lemon-Mint-Honey Dressing.

2. *Sauté sausage:* In a skillet over moderate heat, sauté sausage, stirring constantly and breaking it into moderately coarse chunks, until cooked through and lightly browned, 3 to 5 minutes. With a slotted spoon, remove sausage to drain and cool on paper towels.

3. *Toss and arrange salad:* In a mixing bowl, toss together sausage, orzo, pine nuts, raisins, chopped parsley and chives, and bell pepper with enough dressing to coat well. Arrange lettuce on a platter or individual serving plates and mound salad in center, surrounding with tomato wedges. Garnish with mint or parsley.

MAKES 4 GENEROUS SERVINGS

Szechuan Noodle Salad with Shredded Meat and Vegetables and Spicy Sesame Peanut Dressing

Cold sesame-dressed noodles is a favorite dish in Szechuan-style Chinese restaurants. This version is a great way to utilize whatever leftover meat you happen to have. The ingredients are readily available in Chinese markets and in the specialty-foods section of good-sized supermarkets.

SPICY SESAME PEANUT DRESSING
2 medium-sized garlic cloves, peeled
1 (¼-inch-thick) slice fresh gingerroot
¼ cup packed cilantro
¼ cup Chinese sesame paste
3 tablespoons soy sauce
3 tablespoons rice vinegar
2 tablespoons sesame oil
2 tablespoons smooth unseasoned
   peanut butter
1 tablespoon honey
2 teaspoons Chinese chili oil
1 to 2 tablespoons warm water

SALAD
1½ pounds fresh or frozen Chinese egg
   noodles, cooked al dente, rinsed,
   drained, and cooled
2 cups thinly shredded leftover cooked
   chicken, beef, pork, or lamb
1 cup bean sprouts
6 dried shiitake mushrooms, soaked in
   warm water for 15 minutes, drained,
   stems removed, caps cut into ¼-inch-
   wide strips
2 medium-sized carrots, shredded
2 medium-sized scallions, shredded
   lengthwise and cut into 1- to 2-inch
   strips
¼ cup finely chopped cilantro
6 cups shredded napa cabbage leaves
2 tablespoons black sesame seeds
4 large cilantro sprigs

1. *Make dressing:* In a processor with the metal blade, process garlic, ginger, and cilantro until very finely chopped, scraping down work bowl as necessary. Add remaining ingredients, except water, and process until smooth. Pulse in just enough water to give a pourable, but still thick, consistency. Cover and leave at room temperature.

2. *Tossing and serving:* In a large mixing bowl, combine noodles, shredded meat, bean sprouts, mushrooms, carrots, scallions, and chopped cilantro. Toss with enough dressing to coat well. Arrange a bed of napa cabbage on a platter or large individual plates, mound salad on top, and garnish with black sesame seeds and cilantro sprigs.

MAKES 4 GENEROUS SERVINGS

Veal Tortellini Salad with Peppers, Pine Nuts, and Basil Pesto Vinaigrette

Among the most widely available of fresh or dried filled pastas, veal tortellini make an excellent cold pasta salad combined with roasted peppers, crunchy pine nuts, and a dressing aromatic with fresh basil.

BASIL PESTO VINAIGRETTE
See Index

SALAD

10 cups cooked veal tortellini, al dente, rinsed, drained, and cooled (about 2 pounds uncooked)

½ cup pine nuts, toasted (see Index)

2 medium-sized heads Belgian endive, cut crosswise into ¼-inch-thick slices

1 large red bell pepper, roasted, peeled, stemmed, seeded (see Index), and torn into ¼-inch-wide strips

1 large yellow bell pepper, roasted, peeled, stemmed, seeded (see Index), and torn into ¼-inch-wide strips

1 medium-sized red onion, sliced thin

24 small radicchio leaves

4 firm ripe Roma tomatoes, cored and cut into ¼-inch-thick slices

Fresh basil leaves

1. *Make dressing:* See Index for Basil Pesto Vinaigrette.

2. *Toss and arrange salad:* In a mixing bowl, toss tortellini, pine nuts, endive, peppers, and onion with enough dressing to coat. Arrange radicchio leaves around edge of a platter or individual serving plates. Mound salad in center. Arrange tomato slices around side. Garnish with basil leaves.

MAKES 4 GENEROUS SERVINGS

Lamb Tabbouleh Salad

Based on the dried cracked wheat known as bulgur—a product available in well-stocked supermarkets and Middle Eastern groceries—tabbouleh is traditionally a side salad aromatically seasoned with olive oil, lemon juice, garlic, tomatoes, scallions, parsley, and fresh mint. Since all these ingredients go wonderfully with lamb—another Middle Eastern standard—it seemed only logical to transform tabbouleh into this delightful main-course salad.

2½ cups dry bulgur
2 cups thinly sliced cooked lamb
1½ cups finely chopped fresh parsley
1½ cups finely chopped scallions
1 cup finely chopped fresh mint
6 medium-sized tomatoes, cored, halved, seeded, and chopped fine
2 medium-sized pickling cucumbers, chopped coarse
1 green bell pepper, halved, stemmed, seeded, and cut into ¼-inch dice

⅔ cup olive oil
⅔ cup lemon juice
2 medium-sized garlic cloves, chopped very fine
½ teaspoon salt
½ teaspoon white pepper
24 small to medium-sized romaine lettuce leaves
Fresh mint sprigs

1. *Soak bulgur:* Put bulgur in a mixing bowl and add cold water to cover by about 1 inch. Soak for 20 minutes. Pour contents of bowl into a fine strainer; rinse and dry bowl. A handful at a time, firmly squeeze water from the bulgur, returning squeezed grain to the bowl.

2. *Toss and arrange salad:* Add lamb, parsley, scallion, mint, tomatoes, cucumbers, and bell pepper to bulgur; toss well. In a separate bowl, stir together olive oil, lemon juice, garlic, salt, and pepper; pour over bulgur mixture and toss again until evenly coated. Arrange romaine leaves like spokes around a platter or individual serving plates. Mound salad in center. Garnish with mint sprigs.

MAKES 4 GENEROUS SERVINGS

Macaroni Salad with Ham, Roasted Peppers, Gruyère, and Dijon Mustard Mayonnaise

This main-course variation on a deli-style macaroni salad includes the satisfying additions of baked ham, red bell peppers, and cubes of Gruyère cheese. Still, I've kept the dressing to a simple mayonnaise so that the salad doesn't lose touch with its origins.

DIJON MUSTARD MAYONNAISE

1⅓ cups mayonnaise

3 tablespoons coarse-grained Dijon-style mustard

SALAD

10 cups cooked macaroni (about 1¼ pounds dry), al dente, drained, rinsed, and cooled

½ pound baked ham, cut into ½-inch cubes

½ pound Gruyère cheese, cut into ½-inch cubes

2 large celery stalks, cut crosswise into ¼-inch-thick slices

1 large green bell pepper, roasted, peeled, stemmed, seeded (see Index), and torn into ¼-inch-wide strips

1 large red bell pepper, roasted, peeled, stemmed, seeded (see Index), and torn into ¼-inch-wide strips

6 cups thinly shredded romaine lettuce leaves, chilled in refrigerator

¼ cup coarsely chopped Italian parsley

1. *Make dressing:* Stir together mayonnaise and mustard. Set aside.

2. *Prepare and assemble salad:* In a mixing bowl, combine all salad ingredients except romaine lettuce and parsley. Toss well with enough dressing to coat. Spread romaine on a large platter or individual serving plates and arrange salad on top. Garnish with parsley

MAKES 4 GENEROUS SERVINGS

Chinese Rice Noodle Salad with Slivered Pork, Crisp Asparagus, and Lemon–Sesame Seed Dressing

If you have any leftover pork or ham this recipe is a great way to use it up. You'll find Chinese rice noodles in Asian markets and in the specialty-foods section of good-sized supermarkets.

LEMON–SESAME SEED DRESSING
6 tablespoons sesame oil
6 tablespoons peanut oil
¼ cup lemon juice
3 tablespoons sesame seeds, toasted (see Index)
1 tablespoon soy sauce

SALAD
1 pound Chinese rice noodles, cooked al dente, drained, rinsed, and cooled
1 pound leftover cooked pork or ham, cut into thin slivers
½ pound asparagus, cut diagonally into ¼-inch-thick slices, boiled until tender-crisp, drained, and rinsed
4 medium-sized scallions, sliced thin crosswise
¼ cup finely chopped cilantro
12 large iceberg lettuce leaves
Cilantro sprigs

1. *Make dressing:* Put all the ingredients in a container with a tight-fitting lid. Shake well.

2. *Toss and arrange salad:* In a mixing bowl, toss noodles, ham, asparagus, scallions, and cilantro with enough dressing to coat. Arrange lettuce leaves on a platter or individual serving plates. Mound salad in center. Garnish with cilantro sprigs.

MAKES 4 GENEROUS SERVINGS

Deli Pasta Salad
with Honey-Mustard-Dill Vinaigrette

I like to think of this as the salad equivalent of a deli buffet tray. In fact, it's a good way to use up deli leftovers.

HONEY-MUSTARD-DILL VINAIGRETTE

2 tablespoons white vinegar
2 tablespoons lemon juice
2 teaspoons dry mustard
½ tablespoon dried dill
¼ teaspoon salt
1½ tablespoons honey, at room temperature
¾ cup vegetable oil

SALAD

10 cups cooked egg noodle ribbons (about 1¼ pounds dry), al dente, rinsed, drained, and cooled
¼ pound thinly sliced lean corned beef, cut into ½-inch-wide strips
¼ pound thinly sliced lean pastrami, cut into ½-inch-wide strips
¼ pound thinly sliced kosher salami, cut into ½-inch-wide strips
¼ pound thinly sliced roast turkey breast, cut into ½-inch-wide strips
¼ pound thinly sliced rare roast beef, cut into ½-inch-wide strips
2 large kosher-style dill pickles, halved lengthwise, then cut crosswise into ¼-inch-thick pieces
2 medium-sized carrots, shredded coarse
¾ cup pitted black olives, cut in halves
½ cup coarsely chopped fresh parsley
12 large iceberg lettuce leaves
12 cherry tomatoes
Parsley sprigs

1. *Make dressing:* In a bowl, stir together vinegar, lemon juice, mustard, dill, and salt until smoothly blended. Stir in honey until dissolved. Whisking continuously, very slowly pour in vegetable oil until blended.

2. *Toss and arrange salad:* In a large mixing bowl, combine noodles with other salad ingredients, except for lettuce, tomatoes, and parsley sprigs. Toss well with enough dressing to coat. Arrange lettuce leaves on a platter or individual plates and mound salad in center. Garnish with cherry tomatoes and parsley sprigs.

MAKES 4 GENEROUS SERVINGS

Antipasto Pasta with Herbed Parmesan Vinaigrette

It makes perfect sense—not to mention that it tastes wonderful—to combine a selection of favorite Italian antipasto ingredients with cooked pasta to make a hearty luncheon salad.

The salad can be prepared and tossed with its dressing several hours ahead of time, to be arranged on its bed of crisp romaine just before serving.

HERBED PARMESAN VINAIGRETTE
¾ cup plus 2 tablespoons olive oil
¼ cup balsamic vinegar
2 tablespoons grated Parmesan cheese
2 tablespoons lemon juice
½ teaspoon dried oregano, crumbled
¼ teaspoon dried rosemary, crumbled

SALAD
10 cups cooked plain or multicolored rotini (spiral-shaped) pasta (about 1¼ pounds dry), al dente, drained, rinsed, and cooled

½ pound pepperoni sausage, peeled and cut into ⅛-inch-thick slices

½ pound thinly sliced prosciutto, cut into thin julienne strips

¼ pound mozzarella cheese, cut into ½-inch cubes

¼ pound provolone cheese, sliced thin and cut into ¼-inch-wide strips

1 large green bell pepper, roasted, peeled, stemmed, seeded (see Index), and torn into ¼-inch-wide strips

1 large red bell pepper, roasted, peeled, stemmed, seeded (see Index), and torn into ¼-inch-wide strips

1 (6-ounce) jar marinated artichoke hearts, drained, rinsed, and cut into ¼-inch-thick slices

¾ cup Italian-style marinated black olives, pitted and halved

¾ cup cherry tomatoes, cut in halves

12 small whole pepperoncini (Italian pickled peppers), drained

1 small red onion, sliced very thin

6 cups thinly shredded romaine lettuce leaves, chilled in refrigerator

¼ cup coarsely chopped Italian parsley

1. *Make dressing:* Put all dressing ingredients in a jar with a tight-fitting lid. Shake well and set aside.

2. *Prepare and assemble salad:* In a mixing bowl, combine all salad ingredients except romaine and parsley. Toss well with enough dressing to coat. Spread romaine on a large platter or individual serving plates and arrange salad on top. Garnish with parsley.

MAKES 4 GENEROUS SERVINGS

6
VEGETABLE SALADS

Caesar Salad with Double-Blanched Garlic Caesar Dressing

Classic Wilted Spinach Salad with Hot Bacon Dressing

Nouvelle Wilted Baby Spinach Salad with Enoki Mushrooms, Pine Nuts,
Raspberries, and Warm Raspberry Vinaigrette

Broiled Tofu Salad on a Bed of Spinach with Lemon-Sesame-Ginger Dressing

Sautéed Mushroom Salad with Fresh Goat Cheese and Basil

Baba Ghanoush Salad with Tomatoes, Roasted Peppers,
Goat Cheese, and Crisp Pita Wedges

Indonesian Gado-Gado Salad with Tofu, Mixed Vegetables,
and Hot Peanut Dressing

Grilled Marinated Vegetables with Baby Lettuces, Balsamic Vinaigrette,
and Bread Crumb–Parmesan–Pine Nut Topping

Italian Crudités with Bagna Cauda Dip

Baby Vegetable Crudités with Herbed Aioli and Balsamic Vinaigrette Dips

Caesar Salad with Double-Blanched Garlic Caesar Dressing

While this version of Caesar salad basically hews to the classic line, I've taken one liberty: making the dressing with garlic cloves that have been blanched twice in milk, which softens the raw garlic's harsh bite without any significant loss of its distinctive flavor.

DOUBLE-BLANCHED GARLIC CAESAR DRESSING
3 medium-sized garlic cloves, crushed
1½ cups milk
4 anchovy fillets
3 tablespoons lemon juice
1 tablespoon Worcestershire sauce
½ teaspoon dry mustard
¼ teaspoon Tabasco sauce
1 large egg
½ cup olive oil

SALAD
14 cups coarsely torn romaine lettuce leaves, chilled in the refrigerator
2 cups garlic croutons (see Index)
½ cup freshly grated Parmesan cheese
16 anchovy fillets, drained

1. *Double blanch garlic:* Put garlic and ¾ cup of milk in a small saucepan; bring to a boil, then drain. Cover garlic with remaining milk; bring to a boil again and drain.

2. *Make dressing:* Bring a small saucepan of water to a boil. Meanwhile, in a shallow mixing bowl, mash together anchovies and garlic with a fork or the back of a spoon until smooth. Stir in lemon juice, Worcestershire, mustard, and Tabasco. Drop egg into boiling water; boil 50 seconds, rinse under cold running water, and break into mixing bowl. Whisking constantly, slowly pour in oil until blended. Set aside.

3. *Arrange salad:* Toss romaine, croutons, and Parmesan with enough dressing to coat well. Arrange on individual plates or in serving bowls. Garnish with anchovies.

MAKES 4 GENEROUS SERVINGS

144

Classic Wilted Spinach Salad
with Hot Bacon Dressing

It doesn't seem so long ago that everyone I knew who loved dining out was talking about the fabulous concept of a main-course salad of fresh spinach leaves, wilted on contact with its hot bacon dressing. Though the idea seems fairly commonplace now, the salad is nonetheless delicious.

SALAD
12 cups coarsely torn thoroughly washed spinach leaves
3 cups thinly sliced field mushrooms
3 cups garlic croutons (see Index)
4 hard-boiled eggs, chopped coarse

HOT BACON DRESSING
8 slices streaky smoked bacon, cut crosswise into ½-inch-wide pieces
3 tablespoons lemon juice
2 tablespoons balsamic vinegar
½ tablespoon coarse-grained Dijon-style mustard
½ cup olive oil

1. *Arrange salad:* Put spinach in large individual serving bowls. On top, attractively arrange sliced mushrooms, croutons, and chopped eggs.

2. *Fry bacon:* In a skillet over moderate heat, sauté bacon until crisp, 3 to 5 minutes; remove with slotted spoon and drain on paper towels. Pour off all but about 2 tablespoons of fat in skillet. Scatter bacon over salads.

3. *Make dressing:* Just before serving salads, return skillet to moderate heat. Add lemon juice and vinegar and stir and scrape to deglaze pan; stir in mustard until blended. Stirring continuously, gradually add oil. As soon as dressing is heated through, spoon liberally over salads and serve immediately.

MAKES 4 GENEROUS SERVINGS

Nouvelle Wilted Baby Spinach Salad
with Enoki Mushrooms, Pine Nuts, Raspberries,
and Warm Raspberry Vinaigrette

In this updated, vegetarian version of the now-classic hot spinach salad, enoki mushrooms and toasted pine nuts take over the savory, satisfying role of bacon.

SALAD
12 cups thoroughly washed baby
   spinach leaves
3 cups enoki mushrooms
2 cups firm ripe raspberries
¾ cup pine nuts, toasted (see Index)
4 hard-boiled eggs, chopped coarse

WARM RASPBERRY VINAIGRETTE
¼ cup raspberry vinegar
2 teaspoons creamy Dijon-style mustard
½ teaspoon salt
½ teaspoon white pepper
½ teaspoon sugar
¾ cup olive oil

1. *Arrange salad:* Put spinach in large individual serving bowls. On top, attractively arrange enoki mushrooms, raspberries, pine nuts, and chopped eggs.

2. *Make dressing:* Just before serving, heat vinegar in a small saucepan over low to moderate heat. Stir in mustard, salt, pepper, and sugar. Stirring continuously, gradually add oil. As soon as dressing is heated through, transfer to a heated sauceboat and pass alongside salads at table for guests to pour over salads.

MAKES 4 GENEROUS SERVINGS

Broiled Tofu Salad on a Bed of Spinach with Lemon-Sesame-Ginger Dressing

Like any of the salads featuring grilled seafood, poultry, or meat, this recipe offers up a satisfying portion of protein but in the form of fresh bean curd, available in Asian markets and in the refrigerated case or produce section of most well-stocked supermarkets.

LEMON-SESAME-GINGER DRESSING
See Index

BROILED TOFU
2 tablespoons sesame oil
1½ pounds fresh tofu, cut horizontally into 4 cakes of equal thickness, well drained
¼ cup Japanese yellow miso (soybean paste)

SALAD
12 cups coarsely torn thoroughly washed spinach leaves
12 large dried shiitake mushrooms, soaked in warm water for 15 minutes, stems trimmed, caps cut into ¼-inch-wide pieces
1 large red bell pepper, quartered, stemmed, seeded, and cut crosswise into ¼-inch-wide strips
2 tablespoons sesame seeds, toasted (see Index)
½ cup enoki mushrooms
2 tablespoons finely chopped cilantro

1. *Make dressing:* See Index for Lemon-Sesame-Ginger Dressing.
2. *Broil tofu:* Preheat broiler. Brush sesame oil on the bottom of a shallow baking dish large enough to hold all the tofu. Place tofu slices on top. Brush top of tofu evenly with miso. Broil tofu until top is bubbling hot and golden brown, 3 to 5 minutes.
3. *Arrange salad:* In a mixing bowl, toss spinach, shiitakes, bell pepper, and half of sesame seeds with enough dressing to coat. Arrange in beds on individual serving plates. With a spatula, transfer tofu to salads. Strew enoki mushrooms around tofu. Garnish tofu with remaining sesame seeds and cilantro.

MAKES 4 GENEROUS SERVINGS

Sautéed Mushroom Salad
with Fresh Goat Cheese and Basil

I first tasted a hot mushroom salad at Michael's, a restaurant in Santa Monica, California, where owner Michael McCarty serves it up embellished with slivers of Italian pancetta. His version inspired my own, which I top off with fresh creamy goat cheese that begins to melt on contact with the mushrooms.

The ingredients below use regular field mushrooms along with two of the more exotic kinds you're likely to find in a well-stocked produce section. Feel free to substitute any sort of fresh mushrooms you like; you can even try it with field mushrooms alone.

12 cups mixed baby salad leaves (see Index)
¼ cup walnut oil
2 tablespoons olive oil
½ pound fresh large field mushrooms, cut into ½-inch-thick slices
½ pound fresh large shiitake mushrooms, stems trimmed, caps cut into ½-inch-thick slices
½ pound fresh chanterelle mushrooms, cut into ½-inch-thick slices
6 tablespoons pine nuts

2 large shallots, chopped fine
¼ cup sherry vinegar
2 tablespoons lemon juice
¼ cup finely chopped fresh chives
¼ cup finely chopped Italian parsley
½ teaspoon sugar
½ teaspoon salt
½ teaspoon black pepper
2 to 3 ounces fresh creamy goat cheese
2 tablespoons finely shredded fresh basil leaves

1. *Arrange greens:* On individual plates, arrange beds of baby greens in attractive patterns.

2. *Sauté mushrooms:* In a large skillet, heat walnut and olive oils over high heat until very hot. Add mushrooms and sauté, stirring constantly, until they begin to brown, 2 to 3 minutes. Add pine nuts and shallots and sauté about 1 minute more. Add vinegar, lemon juice, chives, parsley, sugar, salt, and pepper; stir and scrape quickly to dissolve pan deposits.

3. *Finish salad:* Immediately spoon mushrooms and pan juices over baby greens. Dot each salad with small clumps of fresh goat cheese, to taste. Scatter basil leaves over cheese and mushrooms. Serve immediately.

MAKES 4 GENEROUS SERVINGS

Baba Ghanoush Salad with Tomatoes, Roasted Peppers, Goat Cheese, and Crisp Pita Wedges

A specialty of the Middle Eastern kitchen, the roasted eggplant puree known as baba ghanoush here becomes the robust foundation of a colorful composition of vegetables—accompanied by broiler-crisped triangles of pita bread.

BABA GHANOUSH
2 pounds eggplant
3 medium-sized garlic cloves
⅓ cup lemon juice
¼ cup tahini (sesame paste)
2 tablespoons olive oil
1 teaspoon salt
½ teaspoon white pepper

CRISP PITA WEDGES
4 large round pita breads
¼ cup olive oil

SALAD
6 cups thinly shredded romaine lettuce leaves
6 large firm ripe Roma tomatoes, cored and quartered
1 red bell pepper, roasted, stemmed, peeled, seeded (see Index), and torn into thin strips
1 yellow or green bell pepper, roasted, stemmed, peeled, seeded (see Index), and torn into thin strips
½ pound fresh creamy goat cheese
¼ cup olive oil
2 tablespoons dried oregano
2 tablespoons finely chopped Italian parsley

1. *Make baba ghanoush:* Preheat broiler until very hot. With a fork, prick eggplant in several places. Broil, turning occasionally, until evenly charred, about 20 minutes. Let cool, then peel and cut into coarse chunks. Put ¾ of eggplant in a food processor with the metal blade; add remaining ingredients and process until smooth. Add remaining eggplant and pulse until broken into coarse chunks. Transfer to a bowl, cover, and refrigerate.

2. *Toast pita:* Preheat broiler. Split each pita horizontally into 2 circles. Lightly brush with oil and cut each circle into 8 wedges. Spread wedges on a baking sheet and toast under broiler until uniformly golden brown and crisp, 1 to 2 minutes per side.

3. *Arrange salad:* Spread romaine in beds on individual serving plates. Spoon eggplant puree into center of each plate. Decoratively place tomato wedges and roasted peppers on top. Scatter small clumps of goat cheese over eggplant. Drizzle with olive oil and garnish with oregano and parsley. Arrange pita triangles around each salad.

MAKES 4 GENEROUS SERVINGS

Indonesian Gado-Gado Salad with Tofu, Mixed Vegetables, and Hot Peanut Dressing

This salad was first demonstrated to me by the culinary adventurer Copeland Marks, author of, among several other works on the world's exotic cuisines, *The Indonesian Kitchen*. The element that makes the dish so distinctive is its warm, spicy peanut butter–based dressing. Feel free to vary the vegetables you use; you can even add shreds or chunks of cooked chicken, lamb, or pork if you like.

SALAD

8 cups coarsely torn romaine lettuce leaves

1½ cups broccoli florets, boiled until tender-crisp, drained, and cooled

1½ cups thinly sliced carrots, boiled until tender-crisp, drained, and cooled

1½ cups whole snow peas, boiled until tender-crisp, drained, and cooled

1½ cups whole button mushrooms or larger mushrooms cut into ¼- to ½-inch slices

1½ cups bean sprouts

1 large red bell pepper, halved, stemmed, seeded, and cut into ½-inch squares

¾ pound whole firm fresh tofu, drained well and cut into ½-inch cubes

HOT PEANUT DRESSING

1 medium-sized garlic clove

1 small hot red chili, halved, stemmed, and seeded

¼-inch slice fresh gingerroot

1 teaspoon Indonesian shrimp sauce or paste

1 tablespoon vegetable oil

1 cup crunchy-style peanut butter

1½ tablespoons canned coconut cream

1 tablespoon lemon juice

½ tablespoon soy sauce

½ cup cold water

1. *Assemble salad:* In a large serving bowl or large individual salad bowls, arrange a bed of romaine. On top, arrange the remaining salad ingredients in a decorative pattern.

2. *Make dressing and serve salad:* Just before serving, put garlic, chili, and ginger in a food processor with the metal blade. Process until finely chopped, stopping 2 or 3 times to scrape down the bowl; add shrimp sauce and process until smoothly blended. In a saucepan, heat oil over moderate heat. Add shrimp sauce mixture and sauté, stirring constantly, about 1 minute. Add peanut butter, coconut cream, lemon juice, soy sauce, and half of water; cook and stir until peanut butter melts and sauce is smooth and heated through, adding enough additional water if necessary to achieve a pourable consistency. Pour over salads at table, to be tossed just before eating.

MAKES 4 GENEROUS SERVINGS

Grilled Marinated Vegetables
with Baby Lettuces, Balsamic Vinaigrette, and Bread Crumb–Parmesan–Pine Nut Topping

This wonderful lunchtime entree is perfect for a warm summer's day.

BALSAMIC VINAIGRETTE
See Index

SALAD
4 medium-sized Japanese eggplants, stemmed and cut lengthwise into ¼-inch-thick slices
2 red bell peppers, stemmed, seeded, and quartered
2 yellow bell peppers, stemmed, seeded, and quartered
4 small to medium-sized zucchini, stemmed and cut lengthwise into ¼-inch-thick slices
4 small to medium-sized yellow summer squash, stemmed and cut lengthwise into ¼-inch-thick slices
1 large Maui, Vidalia, Walla-Walla, or red onion, cut into ¼-inch-thick slices
Salt and pepper
12 cups mixed baby salad leaves

BREAD CRUMB–PARMESAN–PINE NUT TOPPING
¼ cup unsalted butter
2 tablespoons olive oil
¼ cup fine soft white bread crumbs
¼ cup pine nuts
3 tablespoons grated Parmesan cheese
2 tablespoons finely chopped Italian parsley

1. *Make dressing:* See Index for Balsamic Vinaigrette.

2. *Marinate vegetables:* Put eggplants, peppers, zucchini, squash, and onion in a large mixing bowl. Add half the dressing and toss well. Cover and leave to marinate for up to 1 hour at room temperature.

3. *Grill vegetables:* Preheat grill or broiler until very hot. Lift vegetables from marinade, season lightly with salt and pepper, and place on grill or broiler rack. Cook until golden brown, 1 to 2 minutes per side. Discard marinade.

4. *Toss and arrange salad:* Toss salad leaves with just enough of remaining dressing to coat. Arrange a bed of leaves on a platter or individual plates and drape the grilled vegetables on top in a decorative pattern.

5. *Prepare topping and serve:* In a small skillet, melt butter with olive oil over moderate heat. Add bread crumbs and pine nuts and sauté, stirring continuously, until golden brown, 2 to 3 minutes. Remove from heat and stir in Parmesan and parsley. Scatter topping over vegetables and serve immediately.

MAKES 4 GENEROUS SERVINGS

Italian Crudités with Bagna Cauda Dip

So rich and complexly flavored is the *bagna cauda*—a traditional Piemontese "hot bath" of truffle-scented olive oil, garlic, and anchovies—that it transforms a platter of crisp vegetables into a very satisfying lunchtime meal. Be sure to serve crusty bread alongside, for sopping up the sauce.

SALAD

1 medium-sized fennel bulb, trimmed and cut into ¼-inch-thick slices

1 large red bell pepper, halved, stemmed, seeded, and cut into ½-inch-wide strips

1 large green bell pepper, halved, stemmed, seeded, and cut into ½-inch-wide strips

1 large yellow bell pepper, halved, stemmed, seeded, and cut into ½-inch-wide strips

2 cups broccoli florets

2 cups radishes, leaves trimmed to 1-inch length

2 cups medium-sized mushrooms

BAGNA CAUDA

3 cups heavy cream

3 tablespoons unsalted butter

3 tablespoons white truffle–scented olive oil

4 medium-sized garlic cloves, chopped very fine

3 (2-ounce) cans anchovy fillets, drained and chopped fine

½ teaspoon crushed red chili flakes

1. *Arrange salad:* Place small sauce bowls at centers of large individual serving plates. Arrange vegetables in attractive patterns fanning out from bowls.

2. *Make bagna cauda:* Shortly before serving, bring cream to a boil in a saucepan over moderate heat; reduce heat and simmer until cream reduces by about half. In a separate saucepan, melt butter in oil over low heat. Add garlic and anchovies and sauté, stirring constantly, until garlic is soft and anchovies dissolve. Add chili flakes. Whisking continuously, slowly stir in cream until smoothly blended. Pour sauce into bowls at center of serving plates; transfer extra sauce to a warmed sauceboat.

MAKES 4 GENEROUS SERVINGS

Baby Vegetable Crudités with Herbed Aioli and Balsamic Vinaigrette Dips

Baby vegetables, once a charming quirk of nouvelle cuisine, have become more widely available in good-sized supermarkets—where a greater cross section of cooks are discovering their delicate textures and flavors. Here, those qualities are featured at their most natural—the vegetables served raw, with a pair of complementary dressings for dipping.

Depending on what is available, feel free to vary the selection of vegetables.

HERBED AIOLI
2 medium-sized garlic cloves
1 cup mayonnaise
2 tablespoons finely chopped fresh chives
2 tablespoons finely shredded fresh basil
2 tablespoons finely chopped Italian parsley

SALAD
12 baby zucchini
12 baby golden squash
12 pencil-thin asparagus spears
12 baby carrots
12 baby beets
12 small button mushrooms
12 whole small Belgian endive leaves

BALSAMIC VINAIGRETTE
See Index

1. *Make aioli:* In a food processor with the metal blade, process the garlic until finely pureed, stopping several times to scrape down the bowl. Add mayonnaise and process until smoothly blended. Add herbs and pulse the machine just until combined. Set aside.

2. *Make vinaigrette:* See Index for Balsamic Vinaigrette.

3. *Arrange salad:* Spoon dressings into sets of separate small sauce bowls; place at centers of large individual serving plates. Arrange vegetables in attractive patterns fanning out from sauces.

MAKES 4 GENEROUS SERVINGS

7

FRUIT SALADS

Fresh Fig and Melon Salad with Prosciutto and Mint Honey Crème Fraîche

Summer Fruit Medley with Ricotta and Raspberry Coulis

Salad of Summer Berries with Tart Lemon Granita

Blood Oranges and Pineapple with Ricotta and Honey

Grapefruit and Avocado Salad with Sweet-Hot Red Chili Dressing
and Aged Goat Cheese

Tropical Fruit Salad with Passion Fruit–Yogurt Dressing

Gingered Melon Salad with Honey Vanilla Yogurt

Pear, Endive, and Stilton Salad with Lemon Walnut Vinaigrette

Curried Fruit Salad with Mango Lhassi Dressing

Fantasia of Exotic Fruits with a Wedge of Ripe Brie

Ultimate Ambrosia

Fresh Fig and Melon Salad with Prosciutto and Mint Honey Crème Fraîche

This light, refreshing luncheon salad is perfect for summer—just the right season to find the very best of the fruits that are featured.

MINT HONEY CREME FRAICHE
¾ cup crème fraîche
2 tablespoons honey, at room temperature
2 tablespoons finely chopped fresh mint leaves

SALAD
1 large ripe cantaloupe or honeydew melon, *or* ½ of each, seeded, peeled, and cut into ½-inch-thick wedges
8 ripe fresh green or black figs, cut lengthwise in quarters
6 ounces thinly sliced prosciutto, cut into ¼-inch-wide strips
1 lime, cut into 4 wedges
4 fresh mint sprigs

1. *Make dressing:* In a mixing bowl, stir together all ingredients. Set aside.

2. *Arrange and dress salad:* Arrange melon slices in decorative patterns on individual serving plates. Place fig quarters around edge of melon at rim of each plate. Drizzle crème fraîche over fruit, or serve alongside. Drape prosciutto over fruit. Garnish with lime wedges and mint sprigs.

MAKES 4 GENEROUS SERVINGS

Summer Fruit Medley with Ricotta and Raspberry Coulis

This casual presentation highlights the best of summer's fruits, surrounding a creamy and satisfying scoop of ricotta cheese embellished with a simple sauce made from fresh raspberries. Feel free to modify the ingredients depending on what's best in your market. Let me just add that I love to use the rare and wonderful Rainier cherries, an ivory-and-red-colored variety that makes a brief appearance for a few weeks in early summer.

RASPBERRY COULIS
1 pint fresh raspberries
3 tablespoons confectioners' sugar
1 tablespoon lemon juice

SALAD
2 cups ricotta cheese
3 ripe freestone peaches, halved and pitted, each half cut into 6 slices
3 ripe nectarines, halved and pitted, each half cut into 6 slices
3 ripe plums, halved and pitted, each half cut into 6 slices
24 large ripe strawberries, hulls left on
1 pint ripe cherries, stems left on
Fresh mint sprigs

1. *Make coulis:* In a processor with the metal blade, puree raspberries. Pass and press puree through a fine strainer to remove seeds. Stir sugar and lemon juice into puree. Cover and refrigerate.

2. *Arrange salad:* Place a generous scoop of ricotta in the center of each serving plate. With the back of the scoop or a spoon, indent a good-sized hollow in the top of each scoop. Arrange the peach, nectarine, and plum slices in a sunburst pattern around the ricotta. Place strawberries and cherries around the sliced fruit. Pour raspberry sauce into the hollows in the ricotta, allowing it to overflow slightly. Garnish with mint sprigs and pass any extra sauce on the side.

MAKES 4 GENEROUS SERVINGS

Salad of Summer Berries with Tart Lemon Granita

On a hot summer's day, this salad offers remarkable refreshment. As the granita melts, it changes from a delightful accompaniment to a chilling sauce for the berries.

LEMON GRANITA
½ cup sugar
1 cup water
½ cup lemon juice
¼ cup finely grated lemon zest

SALAD
12 cups mixed ripe berries (strawberries,
    raspberries, blackberries, boysenberries,
    blueberries), left whole
Fresh mint sprigs

1. *Make granita:* In a small saucepan, stir together sugar and ½ cup of water. Bring to a boil over moderate heat; reduce heat and simmer gently 2 to 3 minutes. Cool to room temperature and stir in remaining water, lemon juice, and zest. Pour into a small ice cube tray without divider, or a small shallow dish, and put in freezer. Every 30 to 45 minutes, remove and stir and scrape with a fork to break up crystals, continuing until well frozen but still slushy. If granita gets too solid, before serving, empty into a food processor with the metal blade and pulse to soften.

2. *Arrange and serve:* In large chilled shallow bowls, arrange berries in attractive patterns. Scoop granita into center of each bowl. Garnish with mint and serve immediately.

MAKES 4 GENEROUS SERVINGS

Blood Oranges and Pineapple
with Ricotta and Honey

At breakfast time at a little inn beside Italy's Lago Maggiore, my wife, Katie, and I were served sliced blood oranges lightly drizzled with honey. That lovely dish has been expanded here into a refreshing luncheon salad with the complementary additions of pineapple and ricotta cheese.

Blood oranges, though most common in the springtime, are becoming increasingly available year-round. Substitute regular oranges if you must.

2 cups ricotta cheese
8 large blood oranges, thickly peeled
   with a knife to remove the fruits'
   outer membranes, cut into ½-inch-
   thick slices
1 medium-sized to large ripe pineapple,
   peeled, cored, and cut crosswise into
   ½-inch-thick slices
2 tablespoons lime juice
¼ cup honey, at room temperature
Fresh mint sprigs

Place scoops of ricotta in the centers of individual serving plates. Surrounding the ricotta, arrange the orange and pineapple slices, alternating and overlapping. Drizzle the fruit with lime juice, then honey. Garnish with mint.

MAKES 4 GENEROUS SERVINGS

Grapefruit and Avocado Salad with Sweet-Hot Red Chili Dressing and Aged Goat Cheese

This simple, light luncheon salad is a study in contrasts both subtle and striking. Grapefruit and avocado are nicely complementary: juicy and refreshingly tart on the one hand, smooth, rich, and creamy on the other. The mixture of lemon juice, honey, and fresh hot chili drizzled over them seems to highlight all those qualities; and the sprinkling of aged goat cheese adds yet another dimension.

If you want to embellish the salad even further, try topping it with a few slices of chilled poached chicken breast or whole poached shrimp.

SWEET-HOT RED CHILI DRESSING
¼ cup lemon juice
¼ cup honey, at room temperature
1 small fresh red chili, halved, stemmed, seeded, and chopped fine

SALAD
16 Bibb lettuce leaves
4 large sweet grapefruit, peeled with a knife to remove outer membranes, fruit segments cut with a knife from between membranes, seeded
3 large firm ripe Haas avocados
2 ounces aged dry goat cheese, grated coarse or crumbled
Cilantro or Italian parsley sprigs

1. *Make dressing:* In a mixing bowl, stir together ingredients. Set aside.
2. *Arrange salad:* Place lettuce leaves in a bed on individual serving plates. Arrange grapefruit segments radiating from center like spokes of a wheel. Halve, pit, and peel avocados; cut lengthwise into ½-inch-thick slices. Arrange avocado slices evenly alternating with grapefruit segments. Drizzle with dressing, or pass on the side for guests to spoon. Sprinkle with goat cheese and garnish with cilantro or parsley.

MAKES 4 GENEROUS SERVINGS

Tropical Fruit Salad
with Passion Fruit–Yogurt Dressing

One great benefit of the culinary revolution we've been through in recent years is the ever-growing availability of fabulous tropical fruits. This salad offers up a vibrant medley of them in a vividly arranged presentation.

The passion fruit dressing gets added interest from the inclusion of the fruit's black seeds, which have a wonderfully spicy flavor and crunchy texture. You have the choice of drizzling the dressing over the fruits, or presenting it as a dip in a small bowl in the center of or alongside each serving.

PASSION FRUIT–YOGURT
DRESSING
4 ripe fresh passion fruit
2 cups plain low-fat yogurt
1 tablespoon lime juice
1 to 2 tablespoons confectioners' sugar

SALAD
1 small ripe pineapple, chilled
2 large ripe mangoes, chilled
2 large ripe papayas, chilled
4 ripe kiwis, chilled
4 fresh mint sprigs

1. *Make dressing:* Cut the passion fruit in halves and, with a spoon, scoop out their pulp and seeds. Stir pulp and seeds together with yogurt and lime juice, adding enough sugar to sweeten to taste. Cover and refrigerate.

2. *Prepare fruits:* With a sharp knife, cut off the top, bottom, and skin of the pineapple; cut lengthwise into 8 pieces and cut hard core from each piece; cut pieces in half. Peel mangoes and cut off flesh in ¼-inch-thick slices from either side of large flat seeds. Peel and halve papayas; scoop out and discard seeds; cut each half crosswise into ¼-inch-thick slices. Peel kiwis and cut crosswise into ¼-inch-thick slices.

3. *Arrange salad:* Arrange fruits in decorative patterns on 4 large chilled serving plates, leaving room at the center of each, if you like, for a small bowl of dressing. Or spoon dressing directly over fruits. Garnish with mint sprigs.

MAKES 4 GENEROUS SERVINGS

Gingered Melon Salad with Honey Vanilla Yogurt

Candied ginger, which seems tailor-made to flatter the inherent sweet spiciness of melons, is available in the baking, Asian-foods, or gourmet sections of most well-stocked supermarkets.

HONEY VANILLA YOGURT
2 cups plain low-fat yogurt
1 small whole vanilla bean
¼ cup honey, at room temperature

GINGERED MELON
1 large firm ripe honeydew melon, halved and seeded, fruit scooped with a melon baller
1 large firm ripe cantaloupe, halved and seeded, fruit scooped with a melon baller
¼ cup finely chopped candied ginger
12 small Bibb lettuce leaves
Fresh mint sprigs

1. *Flavor yogurt:* Put yogurt in a mixing bowl. With a sharp knife, carefully split vanilla bean lengthwise. With knife tip, carefully scrape small vanilla seeds from inside bean into yogurt. Drizzle in honey, stir well, cover, and refrigerate several hours.

2. *Mix gingered melon:* In a separate mixing bowl, toss together melon balls and ginger. Cover and refrigerate 1 to 2 hours.

3. *Arrange salad:* Place lettuce leaves in large shallow individual serving bowls. Spoon melon with its juices into center of each bowl. Spoon generous dollops of yogurt over center of melon. Garnish with mint. Pass extra yogurt on the side.

MAKES 4 GENEROUS SERVINGS

Pear, Endive, and Stilton Salad
with Lemon Walnut Vinaigrette

Pears, Stilton cheese, and walnuts are a classic combination, usually served at the end of a meal. Here I've combined them into a simple main-course luncheon salad that satisfies with its contrasting fresh, rich, and tangy flavors and its crisp, creamy, and crunchy textures.

If you can't find Stilton, substitute another good-quality blue cheese.

LEMON WALNUT VINAIGRETTE
¼ cup lemon juice
1 teaspoon honey
½ teaspoon dry mustard
¼ teaspoon salt
¼ teaspoon white pepper
2 tablespoons finely chopped walnuts
½ cup walnut oil

SALAD
24 Belgian endive leaves
6 large firm ripe pears
2 tablespoons lemon juice
½ pound Stilton cheese, crumbled
½ cup walnut halves, toasted (see Index)
2 tablespoons finely chopped fresh
   chives

1. *Make dressing:* In a mixing bowl, stir together lemon juice, honey, mustard, salt, and pepper. Stir in walnuts. Whisking continuously, slowly pour in walnut oil until blended. Set aside.

2. *Arrange salad:* Arrange endive leaves like spokes of a wheel on individual serving plates. Halve, peel, and core pears, cut lengthwise into ¼-inch-thick slices, and toss gently with lemon juice to coat. Intersperse pear slices with endive. Crumble or dot cheese on top. Spoon dressing over pears, endive, and cheese. Garnish with walnut halves and chives.

MAKES 4 GENEROUS SERVINGS

Curried Fruit Salad with Mango Lhassi Dressing

A hint of good-quality curry powder adds its exotic touch to this sweet-savory fruit salad, which is served with a cool dip inspired by India's answer to the milkshake: a refreshing blend of fresh mango and yogurt.

MANGO LHASSI DRESSING
1 large ripe mango, peeled, fruit cut
  from pit
2 cups plain low-fat yogurt

SALAD
2 tablespoons lime juice
2 tablespoons lemon juice
1 tablespoon curry powder
1 tablespoon honey
2 medium-sized apples, peeled, cored,
  and cut into 1-inch chunks
2 medium-sized firm ripe freestone
  peaches, peeled, pitted, and cut into
  1-inch chunks
1 medium-sized cantaloupe, peeled,
  seeded, and cut into 1-inch chunks
1 medium-sized ripe pineapple, peeled,
  cored, and cut into 1-inch chunks
2 cups seedless green or red grapes,
  halved
12 Bibb lettuce leaves
½ cup shredded coconut, toasted (see
  Index)
Fresh mint sprigs

1. *Make dressing:* Put mango and yogurt in a food processor with the metal blade. Process until smoothly blended. Cover and refrigerate.

2. *Mix and arrange salad:* In a small mixing bowl, stir lime and lemon juices together with curry powder until well blended. Stir in honey. Put fruit in a large mixing bowl; pour curry mixture over fruit and toss gently to coat. Arrange lettuce leaves on individual serving plates and mound fruit salad in center. Spoon dressing over fruit, sprinkle with coconut, and garnish with mint. Pass additional dressing on the side.

MAKES 4 GENEROUS SERVINGS

Fantasia of Exotic Fruits with a Wedge of Ripe Brie

The growing availability in supermarkets and produce shops of unusual-looking exotic fruits inspired this salad, which—in this striking arrangement of different shapes, colors, tastes, and textures—should really jump-start lunchtime conversation. The sharp, perfumed flavor that many of the fruits have is nicely offset by a slice of good, ripe Brie cheese.

Tell your guests that yellow starfruit, also called carambola, is a crunchy tropical fruit noted for its refreshing, slightly tart flavor. The babaco, which looks like a cross between a papaya and a starfruit, has a taste that to some palates seems to combine banana, pineapple, and lemon. The feijoa, or pineapple guava, originated in South America and has a texture similar to that of avocado and a flavor that resembles passion fruit.

Kumquats, though they look like miniature oranges and have a similar taste, don't need peeling; with their sweet skins, they can be eaten whole. Fresh litchis bear only a slight resemblance to the canned variety; part of the delight of eating them is splitting open and peeling off their pinkish-brown, rough, papery skin to reveal the succulent fruit inside.

Of course, kiwis and mangoes need no introduction to most present-day eaters—though baby mangoes are especially appealing.

1 pound ripe Brie, cut into 4 wedges

2 ripe starfruit, cut crosswise into ¼-inch-thick slices

2 ripe babacos, cut crosswise into ¼-inch-thick slices

2 ripe feijoas, peeled and quartered lengthwise

2 ripe kiwis, peeled and cut crosswise into ¼-inch-thick slices

2 ripe baby mangoes, peeled and fruit cut from pit on each side into ¼-inch-thick slices

16 ripe kumquats, left whole

16 fresh litchis, unpeeled

2 limes, quartered

Place a wedge of Brie at the center of each serving plate. Around cheese, arrange sliced fruit in attractive patterns that highlight their shapes and colors. Intersperse with kumquats and litchis. Place lime quarters on each plate for guests to squeeze over fruit.

MAKES 4 GENEROUS SERVINGS

Ultimate Ambrosia

There aren't any marshmallows in this grown-up version of the popular luncheon fruit salad—just peak-of-season produce.

> 1 small ripe pineapple, peeled, cored, and cut into ¾-inch chunks
> 2 ripe freestone peaches, briefly dipped in boiling water, peeled, halved, pitted, and cut into ¾-inch chunks
> 1½ cups seedless green grapes, halved
> 1½ cups ripe red cherries, pitted
> 1 cup coarsely broken pecan pieces, toasted (see Index)
> ½ cup shredded coconut, toasted (see Index)
> 1 cup crème fraîche
> 2 tablespoons honey, at room temperature
> 16 butter lettuce leaves
> Fresh mint sprigs

1. *Mix fruits and nuts:* In a mixing bowl, lightly toss together fruits, pecans, and coconut.

2. *Dress and serve salad:* Pour crème fraîche and honey over fruit mixture. Toss lightly again to coat. Arrange lettuce leaves in bed on a platter or individual plates. Mound salad in center and garnish with mint.

MAKES 4 GENEROUS SERVINGS

INDEX